THROUGH THE FIRE

Traveling the Broken Road to Hope and Healing

LUCY DICKENS

WESTBOW
PRESS®
A DIVISION OF THOMAS NELSON
& ZONDERVAN

WestBow Press books may be ordered through booksellers or by contacting:

WestBow Press
A Division of Thomas Nelson & Zondervan
1663 Liberty Drive
Bloomington, IN 47403
www.westbowpress.com
844-714-3454

Because of the dynamic nature of the Internet, any web addresses or links contained in
this book may have changed since publication and may no longer be valid. The views
expressed in this work are solely those of the author and do not necessarily reflect the
views of the publisher, and the publisher hereby disclaims any responsibility for them.

Any people depicted in stock imagery provided by Getty Images are models,
and such images are being used for illustrative purposes only.
Certain stock imagery © Getty Images.

All Scripture quotations, unless otherwise indicated, are taken from the Holy Bible, New
International Version®, NIV®. Copyright ©1973, 1978, 1984, 2011 by Biblica, Inc.® Used
by permission of Zondervan. All rights reserved worldwide. www.zondervan.com...

ISBN: 978-1-6642-4570-9 (sc)
ISBN: 978-1-6642-4572-3 (hc)
ISBN: 978-1-6642-4571-6 (e)

Library of Congress Control Number: 2021919792

Print information available on the last page.

WestBow Press rev. date: 02/24/2022

Praise for

Through the Fire

As a pastor, one of my greatest joys is to watch God change lives. Lucy is one of those people who became completely changed when she reached the end of herself and found God waiting there for her. She and her husband, Richard, became solid leaders in the church, and their testimony has been an inspiration to so many others. I have full assurance that as her story unfolds, her readers will be encouraged to overcome their own hardships by partnering with a God who specializes in making the impossible possible.

—Dr. Don Wilson, founder of Accelerate Group and founding pastor of Christ Church of the Valley (CCV)

What if the pain from your past is actually a springboard for God's greatest purpose in your future? That's what you'll find from Lucy's story. What she endured is unthinkable, but how God used it is unimaginable. This just might be the book God uses to change the trajectory of your life.

—Ashley Wooldridge, Senior pastor of Christ Church of the Valley (CCV)

Through the Fire is Lucy's story. Well, actually, Lucy is God's story of taking the tatters of abuse and making a tapestry of love. Her hope is that this becomes your story too. For all who have been abused, dispossessed, discarded, or shattered, *Through the Fire* is your path to making meaning out of the pain and beauty from the ashes.

—Mark E. Moore, PhD, author of *Core 52*

From riveting stories to life-giving truth, Lucy invites us into the most intimate places of her journey. With people chasing every way imaginable through the fire, God has given us a gift with this book. Lucy points us to the true healer—to the only one who can restore, to the only one who can give us the peace we all so desperately seek: Jesus.

—Rodney Cox, founder, Ministry Insights International

Lucy Dickens walked through a devastating forest fire, protected only by God's guidance and love, in order to bring her vulnerable story of surrender to life. On one level, her book is a page-turner about all the ways she was brought to her knees by heartbreaking emotional and sexual abuse; mental and physical illness; betrayal and abandonment; and even a horrific hurricane!

But the truly compelling narrative is the one about Lucy's growth as a spiritual warrior, during which she found the courage to face her brokenness, hand in hand with Jesus, focusing her efforts on addressing her own issues and entrusting everything and everyone else to God's care. Taking this unflinchingly honest and inspirational journey with Lucy will likely lead readers to strengthen their faith in God's abiding love and to experience the hope, joy, and peace that passes understanding. Christians need the message that it's healthy to be honest, transparent, and vulnerable, to let our own darkness become visible because whoever thinks that Christians are supposed to be perfect and without a history doesn't know Jesus!

—Wendy Boorn, MC, licensed professional counselor (LPC) and author of *I Thought I'd Be Done by Now: Hope and Help for Mothers of Adult Children Searching for Peace*

To each of you who has walked through pain and brokenness and who is seeking a way out, my deepest prayer is that you find hope and healing.

For my beautiful daughters and the incredible women they are, may you always hold on to hope and be encouraged by the words within.

CONTENTS

ACKNOWLEDGMENTS

First, thank You, Lord, for laying this book on my heart and not leaving me alone about it until I answered your call and penned these words. May You use them in a mighty way. Thank You for Your grace and redemption and for saving me, healing my broken heart, and redeeming my marriage. Thank You for all that is yet to come. I could not have made it through this process without the amazing team of people with whom You have surrounded me to help me do what You have called me to do.

To my incredible husband, Richard, thank you for doing the hard work in your life and our marriage to bring it to the beautiful, whole, and healed place that it is. My love and respect for you is never ending. I love to see your heart for helping men, marriages, and your daughters and the way you pour your wisdom into them. Thank you for the wonderful husband, father, and friend that you are and for always believing in and supporting me.

To my incredible daughters, Alicia and Amanda, my love for you is beyond words. Thank you for your unconditional love and for always supporting me. You both continue to teach me so much! I admire your strength and resilience. Special thanks to Amanda for partnering with me in getting my book ready for publication.

To my mom, dad, and brother, Jason, I treasure each of you. Thank you for loving, supporting, teaching, encouraging, and always pouring into me. I am who I am because of you. Thank you for trusting me with sharing my story.

To my in-laws Chuck and Pauline Dickens, your faith, wisdom, and marriage example have been a light and an inspiration to us. Ron and Tina Dickens, thank you for walking alongside us all along, and Ron, for your mentorship of Richard. Chris and Melinda, thank you for all your love and support. Melinda, you are a mighty powerful prayer warrior!

Thank you to my extended family on both sides; you mean the world to me. I would not be who I am today without each of you. To my aunt Pat Trommater, thank you deeply for your editing and feedback of my book. Chuck, Jan, Nancy, Colin—you have impacted our lives and our business in a mighty way. We are forever thankful!

To Ellie Wilson, my previous assistant and someone who is like a daughter to me, thank you for all your support, encouragement, and feedback with this book and more. Thank you to Danielle Garcia, my wonderful new assistant; you are a treasure and so incredibly helpful to me.

To my treasured friends Rodney and Beth Cox, Brian and Peggy O'Rourke, Paul and Angel Sierpina, thank you for your friendship and community and for encouraging me in this book journey every step of the way. I could not have done it without you. Special thanks to Rodney, for all your wisdom and coaching as an author, and Angel, for your editing help. Thank you to MaryJane Johnson, my longtime friend and confidant, for always standing by me and encouraging me and for your reading and valuable feedback too. Thank you to Kelli and John Ruiz for your lifetime friendship and for inviting Richard's family to church long ago; a mighty ripple effect was caused throughout our family. To *so* many other friends and family who have encouraged me in writing this book, I thank you deeply!

To my home church, Christ Church of the Valley (CCV), Peoria, Arizona, thank you for all your incredible teachings rooted in Christ, for community, and for accountability. Thank you to founding pastor Dr. Don Wilson and his amazing wife, Sue, for their vision and passion, impacting our lives deeply for many years. Sue was the first to read and provide very valuable feedback, critique, and encouragement. Thank you to senior pastor Ashley Wooldridge and his wife, Jamie, for their leadership, teachings, friendship, and encouragement. Thank you to teaching pastor Mark Moore for his incredible messages and knowledge and for giving me advice about my book; thank you and to his wife, Barbara, for reading and giving valuable feedback as well. Thank you to Crystal Van Dyke for her help in feedback and editing.

To my neighborhood small group and women's Bible study group, new and old, I love living in community with you. We have learned and grown so much together. Thank you for all your love, encouragement, and prayers. Some of you were beta test readers, and I value your time and feedback immensely.

To my art community, collectors, and followers, I am eternally grateful to you for your support. Your feedback on my artwork and the impact of my stories gave me the courage to step out and write this book. Thank you, Donna King and Audra Weeks, for sharing your book and your own broken journey and encouraging me to finally seek publishing.

To WestBow Publishing and the entire team, thank you deeply. To Eric Schroeder, thank you for first believing in me and the vision of my book and for all your encouragement. Thank you to Joe Anderson, Lucas Berry, Eric Saxon, Roy McMahon, Tim Fitch, Andy Mays, and the editorial and marketing teams. Thank you to Thomas Nelson and Zondervan for your vision and the opportunity offered to me and others in creating WestBow.

Preface

Beautiful One

Beautiful one, do you know you are loved, that you are cherished?

I've prayed for you, prayed over you, for many years. I have cried out to God repeatedly, "Father, how can I make a difference in the lives of those who live with the pain of their brokenness? Show me how to help heal these broken hearts who are trying so desperately to hold on, seeking a way to face each day's challenges. Help me to encourage those who have walked or are walking through sexual abuse, bullying, broken marriages, betrayal, family dysfunction, physical illness, or abandonment as I have."

My heart aches for all the broken hearts, seeking a way through. Often we wonder, "Where was God is in all of this, does He even hear me?" Yes, He does hear you, and yes, He is here and loves you deeply. He cherishes you and me.

I have walked through all of these trials; I am still walking through some of them. I've had so much brokenness in my life that it's sometimes hard to believe it. But as I look at where I am today, walking closely with God and with the hole in my heart not just healed but overflowing, I am overwhelmed. My marriage has been completely restored, and the love between my husband and me unimaginably was raised from darkness to a place of beauty. We have been able to rise above such a troubled and broken journey.

My husband and I now have hearts that break for troubled marriages; that see red flags pointing to hurt and pain. We both have passion for helping others not to make the same mistakes we made. At times, I think I would like to take back all those mistakes and walk that path differently. Then, I am reminded that without the valleys I have walked through, I would not have learned and grown through them to be the person I am today—a person who cries out to bring light, hope, and encouragement to others.

I want to be a beacon of light on a hill for others as they walk desperate roads. The Bible says that God counts every tear, that none shall be wasted. So I can only give thanks for my journey because without it, I wouldn't know that my strength to survive comes only from God.

I'm not perfect. I don't have everything figured out, and I don't think anyone on this side of heaven does. I fall into insecurities, worry, and doubt, just like everyone else. But thankfully, that happens less and less the more I learn to walk and stand in faith, trusting God to continue leading me on this journey. He has never forsaken me, and I am reminded of that when I look back and see how far I have come.

My purpose in sharing my story is not to provide you with a list of dos and don'ts or how-tos. I seek only the courage to be authentic and transparent, sharing my heart, my thoughts, my struggles, and my triumphs. I pray that in my vulnerability, you will find hope, light, and your own courage. I pray you will see Jesus for who He is—a Savior waiting to bring peace into your life, just as He did to mine; that you will know He is ready to meet you right where you are and walk alongside you on this journey called life. He's already there, you know—waiting, longing for you to open the door.

Write a Book, I Heard

Many years ago, when my marriage implosion was still fairly fresh and the healing was in progress (a broken heart does not heal easily or quickly), I sat in my provoking and motivating women's Bible study, listening and thinking to myself, *These speakers are so real, so powerful. I could never do that—stand in front of so many and speak so courageously.* Yet I yearned to be able to impact hearts in the way my own was being impacted. As I looked around the room at the faces of the other women, I could feel their brokenness, a tear gently rolled down my cheek.

Had it always been there, those deep hurts in so many? I couldn't help but wonder why I was suddenly so aware that what we see on the outside is often very different from what is embedded deep within the heart. I realized that everyone has hurts and disappointments, and my heart began to break for others who were in that dark place I had come through. I cried out to God, "Lord, how might I possibly make a dent in all of this hurt? How can I make a difference when the need is so great?"

Write a book—I heard His response in my spirit.

"What? Write a book? I'm no writer. You cannot be serious!" I answered. Over time, I have had to repent that response. I was no painter either, yet God has pulled amazing talent from inside me to create impactful paintings and their accompanying stories.

I finally relented. "If I am to do this, Lord, You will have to give me the words. I have no idea how to do it or what to say."

Just share your story. I want to use it. His voice was so clear in my heart. After many confirmations that this was what God wanted me to do, I found myself surrendered and stepping out in faith, choosing to overcome my fear and trusting Him to guide my hand as my story was laid out. My prayer is that God will speak to you through the words I share. What a beautiful thing to know that my efforts will be worthwhile for even *one* heart to be healed. Is it your heart that I may help?

I would like to start this journey with you in prayer:

Father help me to open my heart, to be real and transparent, as I share the circumstances and events that have shaped me and impacted my life. Help me to present my story with courage, and may the words You give me point to what You have done in my life. May those who read my words see that healing, hope, wholeness, peace, and joy all come from You, as You turn our mistakes or traumas into triumphs. Prepare each heart to walk with me in this journey of grace—grace for me in my weakness and grace for my loved ones with their own brokenness. Fill hearts with grace for themselves and for those who have been part of their pain. But most of all, let them see Your grace and the love that is waiting for them in You. Thank you, Jesus. Amen.

INTRODUCTION

Through the Fire

Fear Not, for I am with you; do not be dismayed, for
I am your God. I will strengthen you and help you; I
will uphold you with my righteous right hand.
—Isaiah 41:10 (NKJV)

The Tinder Fire Emerges

As the call to write this book was weighing heavily on my heart, my
husband, Richard, was invited to go on a backpacking trip through
Israel with eleven other men, including one of our pastors. They would
experience the Jesus trek, a pilgrimage, visiting the holiest sites filled with
great teachings. God had been doing amazing things in and through my
husband. I sensed that He was preparing Richard for something big. As
soon as he received this invite, I heard in my spirit, *Go up to the cabin alone
and write. Now is the time.*

I had never spent time at our mountain home alone. And this was a
new property, a few miles from our previous one. We had stayed overnight
there only once, and the forest area was even more remote. I wondered how
I would do there, especially at night, all alone in the woods. Yet the call
was strong, so I prepared for a journey of my own.

The day before I was to head up, I received word of a small forest
fire near our mountain communities, down deep in the canyon below.
Richard had left for his trip at that point, and when he checked in, I
shared with him about it. I let him know I would be safe and still planned
to go. The following morning, as I was packing, I heard that the first four
communities had gone under pre-evacuation notices. There were several
communities up there, and these were on the edge of the canyon above

the fire below. Mine was the farthest one back, seven miles from the fire. While I had some concern, I felt so strongly that this was where I was supposed to be. Loading my dogs, Maggie and Peanut, and some of my original paintings that I wished to hang at the cabin, I confidently headed up the mountain.

Upon arrival, I hung my special paintings throughout, poured a cup of coffee, and then settled in to begin writing. Of course, I kept my phone close by for fire updates. I trusted the alert system because, so far, I'd received each update by text message, phone call, and an email from the forest service.

For some reason, an overwhelming peace and calm came over me as the words began to pour out about my early years, reliving my story. A text message popped up—there was to be a fire update meeting nearby that evening. I sighed, thinking, *I suppose I should go.* I admit that I was frustrated, even a little irritated, by the interruption. *If I am called to be here writing at this time, then why is there the distraction of a fire nearby?* Did this mean something? Setting my alarm, I continued to write as long as I could.

Arriving at the meeting, I found the last seat available. Looking around the room at the nervous faces before me, I was surprised there were so many people on the mountain. Residents continued to file in, standing in every available space around the chairs. Somehow, I still felt a deep sense of peace. I thought, *It's going to be all right, I am right where I am supposed to be, doing exactly what I am supposed to be doing.*

The forest service officials explained that the fire was started by an illegal campfire down in the canyon. This was so upsetting to everyone, myself included. Such damage was caused by one careless and senseless act! The fire had spread, but hotshot crews and helicopters were on their way, and the forest service did not expect the fire to jump out of the canyon. The meeting seemed positive and confident, and I left there without worrying.

Returning to the cabin, I wolfed down a sandwich, as I was anxious to get back to telling my story. I filled page after page; the words tumbled out, one after another. Why had I fought this for so long, over ten years in fact? *Lord, please help me to tell my story in the way You would have me tell it. Please impact hearts. You know I never wanted to write a book, and now I seem to have a burning passion within me to write this and get it out there to help others. Only You could put this passion in me where there was none.*

I vaguely noticed the sound of the winds rising strongly as I wrote into the wee hours. I didn't want to stop writing, yet part of me recognized that if I stayed up late, then maybe it would be easier to sleep through the night on the third floor all by myself.

Screaming through the Night—Evacuation

Finally, I headed upstairs with Maggie and Peanut, my miniature dachshunds. I did try to sleep, but the winds kept rising until they were screaming full on through the trees and shaking the windows. Soon after, the eye watering, acrid smell of smoke was strong in my bedroom and throughout the house. Half asleep, I thought, *How on earth can anyone fight a fire in this? Surely it has to be jumping out of the canyon. Lord, please calm the winds, and keep the firefighters safe!* Sleep was impossible. My dogs were running around the room, shaking out of their skins and crying, especially Peanut, who is terrified of thunder and loud noises. His eyes were bugged out as he panted loudly.

I went downstairs with them and put on a movie—loudly—to drown out some of the noise. Of course, this did little to nothing for the smell of the smoke throughout the house. I still trusted that I would receive an alert and had not yet, so it must be OK. *Pirates of the Caribbean* and then *King Kong* bellowed through the cabin as the winds raged outside. There were times when I tried to get a little sleep but to no avail. *Why is this happening, Lord? I know You want me here, writing. How can this be happening now, as I finally write? Is this an attack of some sort, something to keep me from sharing my story and what You have brought me through? Is this a parallel that we will continue to go through crises in our lives? Who knew I would be battling one crisis while trying to write about the ones in my past? What was going on here?*

It was a long night and seemed never ending as it dragged on.

Morning finally came, and I awaited my update. Stepping outside, the smoke was *much* greater and closer, and the winds kicked up furiously again. They were 25–35 miles per hour with gusts to 50 miles per hour. I called the ranger station and was told they were still awaiting the morning update, but they did not think the fire had gotten out of control overnight. *Really?* I thought. With nothing to do but wait, I began my writing again.

Somehow, writing was good for me, distracting me from the waiting—or worrying. The words were still flowing.

My mom has previously planned to come up from Payson, about an hour's drive away from me, to have lunch that day. She was also worried about me and wanted to check on the conditions herself. I stopped typing when she arrived, having lost track of time. I stepped outside and was alarmed to see the big black smoke clouds were much closer. Just then, I received an alert—the first three mountain neighborhoods were under mandatory evacuation. *What?* There were maybe eight or so communities, and as I said, I was farthest from the fire. *Surely, I will be safe*, I thought.

Before long, another warning came of more evacuations. "No! I don't want to leave! I am supposed to be here. I am supposed to be writing!" I cried out to my mom.

Evacuation

We decided we'd better pack up. I did *not* want to leave. Mom and I photographed everything possible, just in case—I was so thankful to my mom for that suggestion. We had started loading the car when word came that all communities were under mandatory evacuation except mine, but I was to get prepared. By the time we finished with the car and had turned off the gas, power, and water, the sky had grown black and orange, and the fire looked *extremely* close.

"We better go!" I said hurriedly as fear rose higher within me.

As we were pulling out, I filmed a video with my cell phone of our hasty escape. It was then I received my evacuation notice. Heading away from the fire toward Winslow, about 40 minutes to the east, we drove through thick smoke the entire way and then headed northwest toward Flagstaff. It was then that I broke; tears streamed down my face. I wiped my eyes repeatedly trying to see through the dense smoke.

There was something oddly comforting about following my mom out of there, with her leading me to safety. Relief washed over me. At that point, however, I just wanted to talk to my husband. It had been two days since our last communication from Israel. Was he OK? He had no idea what had been going on here. I knew he couldn't do anything; I just needed to hear his voice. I called everyone I could think of who might be able to reach him.

Finally, after many hours, I arrived home, exhausted and drained. I could not believe that I had been at my cabin for only twenty-four hours—my, how things had changed. Not long after that, Richard called. I broke down on the phone with him as the experience rolled over me like a tidal wave, yet I was so thankful to hear his voice and to know we were both OK. We prayed for the safety of the firefighters, the people evacuating, and our homes, as well as for a calming of the wind and for the rains to come.

I shed tears and my stomach lurched, nausea was building. Why did everything have to go straight to my gut? It was so frustrating! I headed for my saltines and ginger ale. After a time, I settled back into my writing and wrote well into the night.

The next morning, I learned that 8,600 acres had burned, and the blaze, which authorities were calling the Tinder Fire, had moved into the first community. Homes were lost. High winds were expected again, but a new weather front was moving in. *Lord, may the winds shift away from our communities!*

I was able to Facetime briefly with my husband. Relief flooded my heart when I saw him, knowing that he was OK and was having an amazingly spirit-filled and powerful time. God was moving in them. Next, I started the day in prayer and reading; I was thankful for my many blessings, thankful for the safety of my family and my sweet doggies—they are my family too. I was reminded that although our belongings were special and meant so much to us, they were just *things*.

Nothing is more important than our relationships with the Lord and each other. I gave thanks that the evacuations were effective and had gone smoothly. I prayed that the Lord would keep all the firefighters and emergency personnel safe.

Apparently, this book was to describe my past and present trials. I sure didn't see that coming. It is always amazing how God works. That day, after my time with the Lord, I felt much calmer. Peace came into my heart again.

This too shall pass. I am with you. This serves my purpose.

What? Where did that come from? I learned that when I write, I should put it all down. The Lord spoke to me in that way often.

"What do You mean, Lord? As in the sharing of this new journey, this new trial with others?" I responded.

Having kept a close watch on the updates, I needed to set it all down. I had been doing this all morning, and I couldn't change a thing.

Sometimes, you can make yourself sick. It was time to look back again, get back into my story. Sometimes, you just need to look back to see *all* that God has brought you through, strengthening your faith and resolve, seeing all the answered prayers and how God has moved in those situations. Often, you may not even see it all until you have moved through it and looked at it from behind. God is so faithful; He would bring me through this as well.

Returning to my writing, I seemed to step back into time once again. I walked through those moments that have shaped who I am. I felt myself gaining new insight, even as I wrote those words.

Just then, I received a text from our firefighter friend that the fire was on the southeast side of my subdivision. *No!* My hands shook visibly as I started sending out updates to everyone. My email, phone, and social media started blowing up. I was thankful for so much care and concern, that so many people were praying for us. The outpouring of love was truly incredible. Searching to find every possible bit of information on the fire, I came across a map—and my heart sank. I was not sure how far away it was then—a mile, maybe two? The firefighter said that many were working the line.

Protect them, Lord. Bring them favor.

I had also been in contact via text with a reporter friend at Fox10 News. She asked if they could interview me. Quickly, I threw myself together and started unloading my paintings from the car. Bringing in one beloved memory after another, I realized that a painting was missing, although I was sure I had loaded it! How was this possible? I knew I'd brought it out. I searched everywhere, and my heart began to sink further. Could I have left it in the driveway? *Please, Lord … I hope my mom has it.* These were not just irreplaceable paintings; they were captured memories. Each one I painted was filled with emotion over a specific experience or memory. The missing one, *Hidden Places*, was from a very special anniversary trip at our cabin, with the late-afternoon light shining through the pine trees onto the snow. Another precious one was *Wanna Play?* Not only was it a large painting of Blue Ridge Reservoir, but it also had our beloved Lacy, our late cocker spaniel, on the edge of the rocks, playing with the ducks. How awful it would have been to lose her again.

I got myself together and ate my Ramen, which has always been my go to when I can stomach nothing else. No more news-surfing was going to help me now, so I returned to my story. Being obedient to keep my story flowing was such a huge help to me. This kept my mind occupied and on more important things.

It was then that Mom texted me, sharing that she had the painting. *Amen, thank you, Jesus!* I prayed that my mountain home would still be standing when we returned. I reflected on how thankful I was that we were all safe. Although I did wonder if we should have bought this new big place. The news crew arrived then, and my emotional interview was filmed. Later, I awaited its airing on the evening news.

Searching for news updates again, I found another alarming map—the fire was raging closer to our place. How could this possibly be? It felt so surreal. *Lord,* I prayed, *help them hold this line. Keep it out of these homes. Shift the winds, please! Bring the rain in sooner. Stop this tragedy.* I continued to be thankful for so many prayers and people rallying around me in support. I hardly knew what to do with myself then. I had updated everyone I could think of and had checked every website. Funny—I was meeting neighbors in our mountain community and via the Facebook posts for the first time. We had hardly met anyone yet and wondered how we would. Talk about a wild way to meet your neighbors.

Our time on the mountain always has been so beautiful—a place of healing and hope, family and friends. We had spent a lifetime up there, exploring and playing. Those memories flooded over me—all the special times—but I needed to remember it was not the cabin itself. It was being out in God's creation and enjoying it with the ones we loved. Even if my cabin and its belongings were taken, nothing could take these memories from us.

Now what? I thought. *Do I write more?* I found it harder and harder to concentrate now. My place could be burning at that moment. *Lord, help me.*

My daughter Amanda was coming to be with me that night. I was very much looking forward to her arrival, Not knowing what else to do, I began to pace in earnest.

Finally, Amanda arrived to have dinner with me. She was so compassionate and empathetic and just wanted to be there for her momma. I loved it. I loved that both my girls still called me momma; it tugged at my heartstrings so. I had just gotten off the phone with my older daughter, Alicia, who wished she could be there and give me a big hug. I missed her very much, as she was living in Los Angeles, and we hadn't seen her in three months. Amanda and I shared a pepperoni pizza and watched my news feed and then the evening fire report. It was still not contained, but it appeared the lines were holding and that it had not progressed farther into my neighborhood.

We then turned off the news and watched a silly movie together; it was the best medicine. We laughed and took our minds off things for a while; it was comforting to have her with me. I was tired of being alone.

God, I love my daughters and the comfort they bring me.

I slept that night, *finally*, as I'd taken Tylenol PM. Sleep was often such a battle for me. But I slept and was thankful. I awoke to my little Maggie giving me wake-up kisses early in the morning. I felt unusually calm and peaceful. *Everything is going to be OK.* Alicia called to check on me, bringing me much comfort once again.

The Fire Rages

Grabbing my coffee, I turned on the news and started searching the internet for updates. The first thing I witnessed was video footage flying over the burned-out homes in the closest community to the fire. Twenty or so had burned, mostly on the cliff edges, where the fire had come up out of the canyon the night the winds were screaming and I was smelling smoke in the house.

How strange and eerie seeing homes standing and next door nothing but ashes and stem walls, absolutely nothing left. I received a message from a high school friend, the home in ashes I just watched was her sister's, one we had visited a couple months ago. My how things can change in an instant.

The fire was over 11,000 acres but the fire lines at the communities seemed to be holding. The winds were supposed to shift later that day, which would be away from our cabin. The firefighters felt good about the perimeter they had burned in preparation of these shifting winds. I prayed they would hold and that the wind pushed only into what had already burned and had little fuel left. Rains were expected to come early that evening and bring cooler temperatures, possibly even snow in the night.

Richard tried to FaceTime me then, his image appeared for a split second and was gone, there was not enough signal. Disappointment washed over me, I couldn't wait to squeeze him tight, I missed him terribly!

Our firefighter texted again, he said there were many hot shots in my area. "If there was a threat to your place, the sheriff's office would contact you.", he explained. His own community was the one with the homes burned, and thankfully his home was still standing.

Seeking to calm my heart and anxiety, comforting Bible verses drifted through my mind.

> Do not be anxious about anything, but in every situation, by prayer and petition, with thanksgiving, present your requests to God. And the peace of God, which transcends all understanding, will guard your hearts and your minds in Christ Jesus. Finally, brothers and sisters, whatever is true, whatever is noble, whatever is right, whatever is pure, whatever is lovely, whatever is admirable—if anything is excellent or praiseworthy—think about such things. Whatever you have learned or received or heard from me or seen in me—put it into practice. And the God of peace will be with you.
>
> —Philippians 4:6-9 (NIV)

Many times I have come back to this scripture. By prayer and petition with thanksgiving bring your requests to the Lord, and the peace of God which transcends all understanding *will* guard your heart and mind in Christ Jesus. Dwell on what is true and good and lovely and praiseworthy, and the God of peace will be with you.

I have learned by not controlling my thoughts, they can run away with me causing a giant downward spiral, a rabbit hole that is often hard to climb out of. I've been dragged down this hole more times than I can count, more than I would care to admit. Shifting to a heart space of gratitude is key for me.

Finally, Some Containment

The fire continued to rage with no containment, and the fire line was just a half mile from my place, yet this line had held for a couple of days. The fire was uncontrollable down in the canyon, with no real way to fight it. This canyon wrapped around the far side of our community. A storm front moved in, finally, changing the fire's direction and dropping the wind speed. The temperature fell as well. Then, in the evening, precious rain fell, even light snow. This was such a blessing, and things improved quickly over the next few days. The report finally said 8 percent contained, then 48, then 79 percent.

The edge of the fire by my subdivision took some time before they considered it contained. Then, a couple of days later, they felt secure in letting the residents back into the area in a staged process.

Thirty-three homes had been lost as the fire tore out of the canyon and into the closest communities. Fifty-seven other structures were lost as well. My heart broke for those that lost their homes. Our mountain home was still standing. Gratitude flooded my very being as I realized just how close the fire had gotten. I wanted to race back up the mountainside to celebrate, but I could not.

I had another victory party planned—it was time to pick up my husband from the airport. I asked our newly met neighbors if they could drive by my property and check on it for us.

My Husband Returns

My husband, Richard, sure was a sight for sore eyes. How wonderful to hold him in my arms, with both of us safe and reunited. Over the next few days, he shared his life-changing experience of backpacking through Israel. He described the incredible group of twelve men and the amazing bond they had formed for life. He described all the places they visited of biblical and historical significance, like Masada, Caesarea, Megiddo, Nazareth, Mount Carmel, Mount Arbel—so many holy sites in and around Jerusalem, the Dead Sea. They even visited the Jordan River, where one of the men was baptized.

Richard was emotional and passionate as he shared these experiences. I loved seeing this in him and was so proud. He felt more direction and purpose in what God would have him specifically do.

Not Out of the Woods Yet

Then, just days later, as we were preparing to share his trip with our neighborhood Bible study group, Richard received a phone call from our firefighter. The fire had reignited on the edge of our community. The winds were expected to become extreme again in the coming days. He asked if we had received an alert, and we had not. He was concerned enough to pull all of his construction equipment off our property as he was also the one rebuilding our decks at the time. We clearly were not out of the woods yet, like we thought we were. I wished desperately this would end.

A couple of days earlier, I'd heard that the fire was still only 79 percent contained and over 16,000 acres had burned. How scary, as this was only the beginning of the fire season, and everything was so dry. *Lord, we need slow soaking rains!*

An Alarming Phone Call

While working on a painting commission and taking a writing break, I received a call from Mom: "Have you heard from your dad? He is being flown by helicopter from the Payson hospital down to the valley."

Apparently, he'd awakened early that morning and felt like an elephant was sitting on his chest. He had pains front and back, shortness of breath, and looked gray in the mirror. Dad took a baby aspirin and told no one; he didn't even push the medical alert button I'd just got him. He decided to go work at the Payson rodeo, parking cars. Later, he told my stepdad he was not feeling well; finally, he went to the hospital.

Upon arrival, they performed an echocardiogram, talked to his cardiologist, and immediately flew him down to Phoenix. The doctors said he had a blocked artery. Dad told my stepdad not to say anything to anyone yet. Thankfully, he called Mom, and Mom called me. I called him.

When he got to the hospital in Phoenix, around 1:30 p.m., they rushed him right into the cath lab. He had been in the middle of a heart attack since waking that morning and *still* was having one. Years ago, my dad had a quadruple bypass with many complications, and we almost lost him. The doctor came out and explained that this time, it was in the one artery without a bypass. They were able to put a stint in to open up the artery.

We were told this area of his heart went for so long without blood flow that they would not know the extent of the damage for at least twenty-four hours. In the room, he was lighthearted about it all. The doctor came in and asked him questions. My dad knew it was a heart issue; something similar had happened a few times in the last week or two. He took baby aspirin for it. He hadn't said anything to anyone.

I was sitting there getting angrier and angrier. Arms crossed, I was trying *so* hard not to lay into him for ignoring his symptoms and not telling us. We'd had that discussion before, and I was his medical power of attorney. I needed to know these things.

Later, we learned there did not seem to be major damage. I scolded him a bit for what it put him and us through. He was a very fortunate man; he could have died, without saying goodbye or giving us the chance to say goodbye. He could have died alone. Once again, he had dodged another bullet. As I sat by his bedside, I couldn't help but think, *What's with the current big trials while I am trying to write about past trials, Lord?*

And then there was me; I had been dealing with serious gut issues for over eight months. I had been trying to figure it out for myself and was making dietary adjustments. I was so tired of seeing medical doctors and them often not having conclusive answers. My NMD (Doctor of Naturopathic Medicine) and I and were working on these issues.

Richard—maybe partially sparked by Dad's situation but more so from hearing a doctor interviewed on talk radio, discussing many of my symptoms—asked me to promise to get in for testing. I was in the middle of all those tests and scans while dealing with the fire and my dad's situation. Why was I thinking I could ignore this too? It wasn't the same; it was not as serious—or was it? Off to the doctor I went for further testing.

After the Fire

Finally, after about two weeks, the fire was contained, and we were able to make it back up to our cabin, which, thankfully, was unharmed. As we drove through the affected communities and dropped off supplies to help them, we saw the devastation firsthand. Many homes were completely gone, yet other homes, next to them, stood virtually untouched. There were even green trees standing in between them. The energy as we drove through was eerie and sad. Homes that were lost were nothing more than ash and stem walls and the occasional metal roof; maybe a solitary toilet sat nearby. My heart broke for those people and for the forest so badly scarred, yet I thanked God there were no injuries.

In time, hearts will heal, fear will pass, and the forest will begin anew. Times like that are when we are called to come alongside each other through this healing process. We are not meant to go it alone but to do life in community. Eventual good can come from the other side of a fire, both literal and the traumas we each walk through. The title of my book emerged: Through the Fire, Traveling the Broken Road to Hope and Healing.

And now, on to my story. Walk with me, will you?

As you travel through the following pages, you will find a variety of life experiences and trials, each that taught me something new about the heart and character of God. One after the other, they were woven together, teaching and guiding me. Through all of these mountaintops and valleys, I found hope, healing, and wholeness and became who I am today. It is God's story interwoven throughout my own. It's his story I pray you see within mine.

1

THE ARROWS LODGED DEEP

Their tongue is a deadly arrow; It speaks deceit.
—Jeremiah 9:8 (NIV)

In addition to all, taking up the shield of faith with which you
will be able to extinguish all the flaming arrows of the evil one.
—Ephesians 6:16 (NIV)

The Early Years

Lucy, age five, 1973

As a child, I often felt uncomfortable in my own skin, filled with tension or fear—so many things happened that I could not understand. I felt like a fish out of water, as if I never quite belonged. At an early age, I had already experienced a number of extremely difficult and painful experiences that shaped my young heart, filling it with lies.

My parents met in high school while living in Michigan. During this time my mom became pregnant with me. Coming from a conservative Catholic family in the 60's, this situation brought great shame on the family. However, they did marry, and a couple of years later, I had a little brother. Our family moved to Arizona when I was three and my brother was one. Mom was following her parents, who had moved there just before I was born. What a lonely time that was for my mom, pregnant, newly married and without her family. She believed life would be easier with her mom nearby—a support system as she navigated the challenges of early marriage and motherhood.

It seemed to take forever to drive across the country. "Are we there yet? Are we there yet?" I repeated often. The never-ending road stretched far into the distance and my baby brother cried nearby. It was hard to travel long distances with a little one who didn't want to be constrained for long periods.

The desert seemed such a barren and dry place after leaving the lush greenery of Michigan. Mile after mile, the green seemed to fade to browns and greys. It would be many years before I could see the true beauty of the desert. Finally, we arrived and moved into a small block home in the suburbs, just off a busy street.

Before long, I made some new friends in the neighborhood and prepared to start school. I spent most of my time exploring with my brother in the fields around us, always playing make believe. Mom would share arts and crafts with me, which I loved; she sparked the artist in me, as I would later follow in her creative footsteps.

Brown family, 1972

My parents often seemed to be fighting, and it left me feeling very unsettled. Our home was generally not a home of peace, although my mom always sought to make it so for us kids.

During my young childhood, I was repeatedly molested by an extended family member. I didn't really understand what was happening. I just knew it didn't feel right. He told me to keep it a secret. I felt love for him, and there was nothing mean or violent about what he did, but even at that young age, I knew he was touching me in ways he shouldn't have. At some point, my brother saw what was happening and told my mother. I don't remember her reaction at the time, but as a mother myself, I can only imagine that she must have been horrified.

My dad never talked about it to me, and I wondered if he even believed it then. The next thing I knew, a family meeting was called. My brother and I were sent to play in the other room. "He" was at the meeting, and I wanted to crawl in a hole and die. I was only about six or seven years old, and I knew they were all talking about me, even though I could only hear muffled voices. My skin was crawling. I wondered if I had done something wrong; maybe it was my fault somehow. What would happen next? No one ever spoke to me about what was said in that meeting, and although my brother and I were never allowed to be alone with this individual again, it seemed, to my young heart, like everyone was pretending nothing had happened.

My abuser never spoke to me about what had happened, never apologized, and never admitted he had done anything wrong. Mom tried talking to me about it, assuring me it was not my fault and that I had done nothing wrong. It should have never happened. According to my mom, I would not respond when she talked to me. I could not even make eye contact. I don't remember much of this. It's funny what your mind blocks out under trauma. I trust that her words are true, though.

Despite that, our family was (and is) close-knit and spent a lot of time together. There was much love and laughter between us and still is. The only problem was that my abuser was almost always at family functions when I was young, which filled me with a great uneasiness. The arrows (lies from others that I began to believe and were spun by the enemy) had plunged deep into my heart and began to grow. *I'm dirty. I'm damaged goods. I'm abused. I'm not good enough. There is something wrong with me.* My mother took me to counseling when I was in elementary school, but it was short-lived. I was not ready to talk about it, not until many years later.

Sometime later, when I was eight or nine years old, my abuser was accused of touching another young girl. I don't know if it was true but it was surely possible. He was charged and taken to court, and I was called to testify. I was a scared little girl, sitting on the witness stand in front of all those people—and him. I was asked if he had ever touched me. Fear engulfed me—fear for me and for him, my throat closed. I don't remember being given any coaching. No one told me what to say, but I just could not speak the things that happened out loud—so I lied. How could I say those things in front of all those people? I felt some need to protect him, even then.

Later, as an adult, I talked about this with my mom, but she had no memory of my being questioned in that way. It was at that moment that I was able to put myself in my mom's shoes, to some degree. As a mother, I realized how excruciating that whole experience must have been for her. My heart was not the only one that was wounded through what had happened to her little girl. Years later, I wondered if it could have happened to her or anyone else in the family. Mom and her sisters all talked together and assured each other the answer was no.

I never seemed to fit in at school. I am not sure why, exactly. I was awkward, found it hard to make friends, and was deeply insecure. One day after school, a boy locked me in the bathroom and pounced on me, pinning me to the floor. Terrified, I somehow managed to break free and escape. I have no idea why this happened, but I told no one about it at the time. I figured no one would believe me anyway and maybe I'd done something wrong. Or maybe I thought I shouldn't be a snitch.

Another time, my brother and I, and a friend, were playing in the desert behind our house when an older boy told us to follow him. He wanted to *show* us something. Foolishly, we followed. I was barefoot and had to tiptoe through the sticker bushes until we entered some kind of fort he had made of dried tumbleweeds. There were pages from *Playboy* magazine stuck to the thorns inside the fort. Jason and his friend turned and ran away, but the boy grabbed my arm and pulled me back. Again, in terror, after struggling, I was able to break free. I ran as fast as I could through the desert, crying all the way and arriving home with my feet bleeding. I'm not sure why I never told anyone this either until many years later. Perhaps I thought no one would believe me, that those things that kept happening to me were my fault, or that I would somehow be the one to get in trouble. So much of what happens in a scary world can get jumbled in the mind of a child.

During this time in my childhood, my parents often fought about something—another woman, money, drinking, drugging. My dad had pretty much checked out by then. I don't remember spending much time with him or him really playing with me. We did spend a lot of time camping in beautiful places, though; that was how we chose to spend our family vacations. I enjoyed that; even then, I was entranced by nature, by the beauty around me—the cloud formations, trees, and especially all the pretty flowers—but there often seemed to be tension. I bounced between awe of the beauty of nature and feeling worried and unsettled. Would my parents fight? Would I be picked on again at school? Would the other kids like me? Would they accept me?

On top of everything else, I developed asthma. I remember the suffocating feeling, struggling just to breathe, fighting for air. The oxygen seemed ripped from my lungs. I could not get enough air. I was in and out of the emergency room many times. Looking back, I feel that some of my health issues were born from the stress I had been walking through. I remember lying in a hospital bed in an oxygen tent with severe pneumonia, brought on by my asthma, and thinking that I would know who really loved me by who came to visit me. Of course, my parents came, and my aunt and uncle too, and that meant the world to me.

My aunt and uncle have continued to always be there for every important event in my life and have been such a testimony and witness to me and, later, to the man who would become my husband.

I had to work at removing that arrow that said if I was sick, I would know who loved me by who showed concern, thus inviting sickness into my life to prove it. The lies we believe can feel like arrows that pierce our hearts and stay imbedded there. I believe that the trauma of my childhood affected my body and my health. I have continued to have illness and chronic pain, off and on, throughout my life, and I wonder how much of it is connected to things that happened to me in my childhood. All of what I have shared happened before I was ten years old. By that time, I had come to believe, through those experiences, that men were not to be trusted, that they wouldn't be there to protect me, and that they only wanted one thing from me. My body was dangerous; beauty was dangerous.

Even though I hated the fighting, my childhood was not all bad. We had our good times too. Some of my favorite times were doing art projects with my mom and playing hopscotch with the neighbor kids. I remember the creative and inventive birthday cakes my mom would make; my favorite was a school bus. She also painted an amazing giant butterfly mural on my wall (I still love butterflies to this day) and a Winnie the Pooh on her sister's nursery wall. Her talent amazed and entranced me.

I loved going hot-air ballooning with my dad, as he was a pilot. I loved our family outdoor adventures—camping, exploring, going to my grandparents' cabin in the woods of northern Arizona. I spent a lot of time making forts in those woods with my brother. We would play make believe with princesses, and dragons, and knights in shining armor. How fun it was to escape into that imaginary world. We stood under snow-laden pine trees, shaking them until the freezing snow rained down upon us; laughing the whole time. I loved to curl up under the eaves on the deck with a blanket and my dog Duchess during a thunderstorm. Somehow, I was never afraid of those, even when the windows shook with the loudest *crack-boom*! I loved the grand adventures, exploring with my brother. Times were different then; we kids could roam more freely and safely than today. At least, that's what we thought, but I suppose, looking at my life story, it might not be so true after all.

My dad showed me that he loved me by making some of the most wonderful things. He was a talented woodworker and made an enchanting playhouse for my brother and me. We spent many hours there, pretending and living in a world where things were perfect and "right." My dad also made me a beautifully crafted wooden Barbie doll case that opened up to become Barbie's house. This was my favorite "toy". I knew that my dad loved me in his own way, and I came to understand, much later, that he just wasn't sure of the best way to show his love to me.

My dad was also a gifted photographer and loved spending time outdoors, capturing the beauty around him. Who he was is a part of who I am as I look at the world and try to capture what I see in my own paintings. From him, I also learned organization skills, detailed record-keeping, and courage in public speaking. He was and still is a charismatic guy, the life of the party. But although that could be a good thing, it was sometimes a bad thing.

There was a lot of drinking and drugging in Dad's life, and we were never quite sure what his mood would be when he came home. He was never physically abusive, but he would erupt in bursts of rage, saying horrible things—things I still remember to this day. He did not seem to have a filter. Words can be so powerful and damaging, even more so for children.

My own children have vivid memories of things my husband and I have said to them, and we desperately wish we could take those words back. It's no wonder that the Bible calls us to be slow to speak, quick to listen, and slow to become angry. Words tied with emotion stick with us and can drive those arrows deep into a heart.

My dad loved me in the best way he was capable of, and I love him deeply right back. He has grown and has been filled with remorse over his past mistakes. He became clean and sober when I was a young adult, and this changed a lot of things. It was too late to save his marriage, which caused him great remorse. My parents divorced when I was in my early twenties. They felt it was best for them to stay together until my brother and I were out of the house, which was a noble gesture and one I respect. Yet I'm not sure it was best for us, living amid all that strife and tension. Who knows?

I have learned there are no perfect parents. Mine were not, neither were theirs, and my husband and I have made plenty of mistakes too. We all fall short—every one of us—but we do the best we know to do at the time. I have learned the importance of viewing others through the eyes of grace, just as God has done for me. I remind myself each day that it is not too late to choose to do things differently than I have done in the past. I can choose to love others, instead of blaming them.

Today, my dad is a different man; his heart has softened. This once-impossible man, who I could never imagine coming to faith, now sits beside me in church. It seemed a miracle, and I am so thankful. He has a compassionate servant's heart, volunteering every time he gets the chance. In fact, he's Santa. Not only does he look like Santa with his shape and form, big white beard, and rosy cheeks, but these days he is pretty much Santa year-round.

Santa Dad

He loves bringing smiles, happiness, and joy to those around him. This started many years ago and has become a huge part of who he is. He visits homeless shelters, veterans, care facilities, charities, and more, often for no pay. He was recently awarded the Western Regional Charitable Santa of the year. I love this in him, and he is so good at it! Acting has been a big part of his life. I will admit, however, there are times when we wish we could just be out with Dad and *not* Santa. Then God reminds me that my dad is also His son, and I need to let him do what brings him joy. Richard reminds me too.

Mom was always so patient with my brother and me, always taking time to explain and teach us many things about life. She thoughtfully and lovingly answered our questions, even difficult ones, like about the birds and the bees. She encouraged my creativity and exposed me to many different art forms. She taught me to see the world through the eyes of an artist. Mom is a wonderful painter—creative and talented. She has always been a seeker and a learner, hungry for knowledge, and so supportive of us. She is a gifted massage therapist and a healer and has extensive and practical knowledge about a variety of herbs and botanicals. We think of her as a medicine woman, at times. She is compassionate, a mother hen, and an encourager, and she loved us well. She was a good mom, despite her own sadness and pain, which seemed to be because of the state of her relationship with my dad. Over time, she truly found her inner strength, the power from within.

One day I was walking home from elementary school and was followed by a bully, much larger than me. This girl cruelly said, "All you will ever be is used and abused." I felt like I had been punched in the gut; I couldn't breathe. The arrows lodged deeper. How could she have known? How could she have seen that this was the same broken record I'd played over and over in my own mind? I felt like what she was saying must surely be true.

She even asked me, "Where do you want to be punched, in the head or the stomach?" tears streamed down my face.

All I could think to say was, "Neither, you can't because I have asthma." Which was a ridiculous response to an impossible situation, but she did turn and walk away.

When I was nine, we moved to a different neighborhood, a better one. For me, it meant a new school and new friends.

Lucy and Jason, 1978

Somehow, I managed to get off on the wrong foot again. I don't know what I did wrong, but some of the popular girls decided they hated me and made that clear in the way they spoke to me and laughed at me in such a condescending way. Soon, the popular boys joined in, my heart sank even deeper. Oh, the hurtful things they said to me, lodging more arrows deep into my heart. I never knew what it was that earned me such treatment. I did find friends, but I was still uncomfortable in my own skin, believing that I was damaged goods, never good enough. I couldn't wait to get to high school and the hope of a new start.

One thing I have learned over time is that hurting people hurt people. We are all products of our brokenness. With each of those who have hurt me in the past, I have learned, as an adult, to look deeper. What life experiences made them who they are? How did they come to act and react in the way that they did? This realization came from my having to explore and investigate these things in my own life. What shaped me? What lies have I believed? What hurts have I tried to mask? How have all these things impacted how I think, act, and react?

Learning someone's backstory can help to understand that person better. It doesn't excuse their actions, but it can help me to understand how they became broken. Whether it was the one who molested me, other offenders, or the children who were cruel to me, this has helped me to deal with my feelings about what was done or said. I remember that each person has his or her own brokenness. All of our experiences shape us, for better or for worse. However, if we live our lives by blaming others, our own growth will stagnate, and we will deprive ourselves of the abundant joy of living and loving in the present. To break the cycle of hatefulness and abuse, we must put a stake in the ground and make a choice to take responsibility for our own actions and to do things differently.

In his book *A Family Shaped by Grace* , Gary Morland says this:

> It takes a whole lot of courage to face who we are, and a great deal of responsibility to deal with it. It only matters if you want an excuse for not taking responsibility for yourself. It's helpful to understand the things that have contributed to your story, to what happened in your family upriver. These things may help to explain who you are today. But it is your fault alone if you allow those circumstances to keep you from being all you can be. You can stop the chain reaction. Accept your family (or lack thereof one) as with God's overall will for you and accept your ability and promise to use it for good. (2017)

Teen Angst

The summer after eighth grade, my parents separated and shipped my brother and me to Michigan to stay with our grandparents and our aunt and uncle. We didn't really know or understand they were separating at the time. My dad's mom was a harsh and abrasive woman; maybe that is why Dad could be also. She was often blunt and lacked tact. I walked on eggshells around her. She scolded me, saying I wore my feelings on my fingertips and had better stop or they were going to get stomped on.

My aunt and uncle had a place in the country, and we had such fun staying there. The first night, as we tried to sleep on the hide-a-bed, we were dive-bombed by a firefly—the first one we had ever seen. It was magical! We continued to see fireflies, but they never stopped filling me with wonder. We helped on the land, picking wild raspberries and blackberries and tasting them for the first time, their sweetness dripping from our fingertips. We drove the riding lawn mower and later went down to the creek and watched the graceful deer cross. I was entranced by them, but not by the horseflies and other insects that tried to eat us alive! I was bitten right in the middle of my pigtail part, as my scalp was well exposed.

Occasionally, our aunt and uncle would drive us into town and let us go to the arcade to play Centipede and Pac Man (I'm seriously dating myself now). Sometimes, I would watch my little cousins while my aunt and uncle worked on building their house. We returned to Arizona after the summer. Mom picked us up from the airport; she was tan and wearing a vibrant tropical jumpsuit, having been to Hawaii. I was in an uptight tan skirt and shirt with the neckline up to my chin, and my beautiful hair was burned from over perming—all my grandmother's doing. I was struck by the severe contrast between us in that moment, and I looked forward to getting back to myself. My parents did get back together, but not much changed after their time apart.

Starting high school was better, partly because there were so many new kids. I started to come into my own, reinventing myself in a way. But on the inside, I was still paralyzed by insecurity at times. I believed I was not pretty enough, cool enough, or liked enough. I started going to parties where we would drink. It's no surprise that I lost my virginity at a young age. I didn't want to, but what I wanted never seemed to matter. I was starved for affection and attention, and I wanted desperately for someone to love me. A teenage boy wanted sex and would not take no for an answer, so I finally gave up the fight. I felt it was pointless to resist; it was going to happen whether I wanted to or not. I believed that was what I had to do to get and keep a boyfriend, to be loved.

And did he love me? No, he was off to the next best thing. Why did I think I could do no better? I felt so pathetic, so desperate on the inside, and dirty. As women, don't our hearts cry out, "Am I pretty? Am I loved? Am I safe? Am I strong enough?" I was seeking approval and love. This approval became important to me. I just didn't understand that I was looking in the wrong place. Too easily, I caved to peer pressure, sneaking out of my house because my friends, or boyfriends, wanted me to and wouldn't let it go.

We threw a few parties when my parents were out of town although I never got away with it. I knew it was wrong and didn't want to do it, but I so easily caved to peer pressure. After one party that got out of control, I made sure we put everything back and cleaned perfectly. My parents did not suspect a thing—until Dad took the trash out and found it full of empty bottles and cans. Oops!

My brother got into his own kind of trouble. There were a number of instances related to his playing with fire. He was entranced by it. One time, he lit an empty dog food bag on fire and threw it over the wall into the neighbor's yard. Another time, a police officer came to the door, wanting to take my brother downtown. Mom and Dad were not home, so I argued with the officer, saying that it was not necessary to take my brother.

"I will handle it," I told him, "and *I* will tell our parents."

After a while, the cop started to laugh and conceded. "You should be a mediator or something," he said. Situation averted!

I love my brother deeply. Things have been a challenge for him over the years. He's always wanted to be married and have his own babies, but things have not yet worked out quite the way he hoped. He became an incredible high school teacher, teaching high-level math classes and physics. He has been a talented and encouraging track coach as well. My brother pours so much of himself into the students he teaches and makes a huge impact on their lives that lasts for years. I am so proud of him and the way he positively influences so many young lives.

Another boy from my past did a great job of piercing my heart with arrows—the arrows that told me I was dirty, damaged, and powerless. He forced himself on me on more than one occasion, refusing to take no for an answer. There was a time when I was having my menstrual period, and I made it clear that I didn't want to have sex. I fought him hard, but we were all alone on the desert floor, and he took what he wanted. Another time, there was a different young man, and it happened at a party. I was devastated and humiliated.

Why is it still so hard to say I was raped? Somehow calling it *date rape* or *taking advantage of me* sounds better. Why? Is this because I wasn't a stranger to them, and I wasn't badly beaten with it? I was taken against my will after repeatedly saying no. I was forced to have sex and did fight back. Here is where my mind would go: maybe I didn't fight back hard enough, maybe I was not strong enough, maybe it was somehow my fault. The lies run deep.

I was growing into my looks by this point, yet I still found plenty of fault in the mirror, just as I can today. But there were those who felt I was pretty, even beautiful. On one hand, I loved the new attention. I was so starved for approval, especially from men. On the other hand, it scared me, and experience told me it was dangerous. *Boys only want one thing. Keep them at an arm's distance. Don't let anyone too close. They will only hurt you and use you.*

I began modeling in high school. I found validation and acceptance in the fact that others felt I was pretty enough to model. Yet I soon learned how quickly and harshly I was evaluated on my looks in that business. I watched models being constantly criticized for being too tall, too short, too skinny, too fat—the list goes on. Why was it so important to me? Why did I want it so badly? Did I have something to prove? Was I trying to find out who I really was? I participated in a lot of runway shows. Even after I had married and moved to Kentucky, I was hired for print work and a country music video.

Modeling in Tennessee, 1989

I stopped modeling when I became pregnant with my first baby, and after a time, it just wasn't important to me anymore. Modeling was like living under a microscope; there was so much judgment. This all added to my negative body-image issues and critical eye in the mirror.

While I was in high school, I began having extreme bouts of gut pain, attacks that had me doubled over. It felt like a knife blade plunged through my stomach. I would vomit and curl up in a fetal position, shake for hours, and writhe in pain as I waited for it to pass. After an episode, I would have to live on saltines and Sprite, baked potatoes, Cream of Wheat, and of course Ramen. These attacks left me exhausted and drained. They also seemed to come most often after or during extremely difficult emotional times. After many tests, I was diagnosed with irritable bowel syndrome (IBS), which might have been a catch-all diagnosis. Whether that diagnosis was accurate or not, the bouts continued to plague me throughout much of my life.

There was a time in my teen years that I began to jump in the middle of my parents' fights. Somehow, I felt I needed to defend my mother. Did I think she could not handle herself, could not stand up to my dad on her own? I'm not sure what I thought, but looking back, I know it was completely wrong of me to be so mouthy and disrespectful to my dad. In my mind, I felt he did not deserve respect because he didn't give respect. During the time I was dating my future husband, Richard, he witnessed an encounter between my dad and me.

Richard was shocked by my behavior. "If I talked to my dad the way I just saw you talk to yours, my dad would have clocked me good."

While I was all about getting in my dad's face and starting a yelling match, my brother dealt with things completely different. He would do anything he could to disappear into the wall and avoid confrontation. Unfortunately, when I got into trouble, he was often dragged out of bed and lectured right along with me. My parents would say I was strong willed and vocal. It was true and still is, yet I harbored deep insecurities at the same time.

I know now that we are called to honor our mothers and fathers. I understand that we are to honor and respect, whether we feel they deserve it or not. It makes no difference whether we agree with them, whether we perceive them as right or wrong, or whether they have the same beliefs as we do. The Bible says we are to honor them. It hurts to think about how different my relationship with my father could have been if I had truly honored and respected him when I was young.

If you are truly in a physically or sexually abusive situation, things are different. Please seek help immediately.

Reference

1. Morland, Gary. 2017. *A Family Shaped by Grace: How to Get along with the People Who Matter Most.* Grand Rapids, MI: Revell.

2

A Bride-to-Be

A perfect marriage is just two imperfect people
who refuse to give up on each other.
—Dave Willis

What greater thing is there for two human souls, than to feel that they
are joined for life - to strengthen each other in all labour, to rest on each
other in all sorrow, to minister to each other in all pain, to be one with
each other in silent unspeakable memories at the moment of the last.
—George Eliot

I met my future husband in our senior year of high school. Who could
have known that cute, funny guy across the classroom would someday be
celebrating thirty-three years of marriage with me? So close and so much
in love. Even so, it was a turbulent journey to get to that point, and we
have weathered many storms along the way.

Lucy and Richard, high school, 1985

It was the first day of school in 1985, big hair and all. And oh, I did have the *big* hair, red lipstick, leopard-print mini-dress, and red pumps. (Don't judge me; it was the 80s, after all!)

Richard Dickens walked in the room, sat down, took one look at me, and said, "Wow!" (I'm paraphrasing; his word was a bit more colorful.)

"Mr. Dickens, we will have none of that language in my classroom," the teacher said.

"What? What did I say?" he replied.

"You know what you said," the teacher said.

"All I said was wow—but look at her!"

"I understand, but you still cannot speak that way in here," the teacher replied.

I must have turned three shades of red.

From that day on, he carried my books to my car, and eventually, he asked me out. He later described me as one of the hot, popular girls he'd had his eye on for a while but did not have the courage to ask out. I wasn't. I certainly didn't see myself that way, *then or now*. Truthfully, it was hard for me to even type those words. We had a date to go out after a football game. I wasn't sure about being alone with him, so I had two girlfriends with me for back-up. The four of us were heading to a party after the game. He didn't know that we girls had been talking about him during the game. I asked my friend what she thought of him, and she told me that he was going out with her friend from another school, that her friend was wearing his class ring. *Oh, really?*

In the car together, we asked where his ring was. Richard quickly said he did not wear it on game days. After the party, when we were alone, he asked me out again.

I said, "Bring me your class ring, and we will go out. I don't date another girl's boyfriend."

The next day, he showed up with it. I learned much later that he had gone right over and broke up with the other girl. She pitched the ring into a cotton field, and he had to find it before coming to my house.

We dated throughout senior year, and despite our ups and downs, I fell for him hard. We broke up a couple of times, the last time right before our senior trip to Hawaii. How convenient for him with all the girls that would be there, why be attached? On that trip as we talked, I decided I'd had it. I told him I was sick of this rollercoaster. I was through. I didn't want to be with him anymore anyways. That changed something in him, and he fought hard to win me back. After that, we became pretty serious; he bought me a promise ring, which was a popular thing to do back then.

Richard was an athlete—a wrestler and a football player. He partied very hard; he had started young with older brothers and cousins. I partied right along with him. His dad worked out of town most of the time, but when he was home, they had some friction about this.

His dad said to Richard one day. "Where are you moving after graduation? You're not going to live here." That year, his Christmas gift was luggage.

Richard joined the army that same day, shocking us all. He was the last person you thought would. We graduated high school in May, and he left in October of that year.

The drill sergeants pushed the guys to break up with their girls, saying they would not wait for you anyway. "Your girl will be with your best friend before you know it." They wanted these guys to stay focused. Richard tried somewhat to break up with me, but I assured him I would wait. While he was in basic training, he called me and asked me to marry him. This was such a surprise—I felt like he was pushing me away one minute and asking me to marry him the next minute.

"I have to think about it," I told him—which he *still* hasn't let me forget. I wanted both of us to be sure that was what we wanted.

Off to Kentucky

The next day, I called him and told him yes. We were married nine months later and moved to Fort Campbell, Kentucky. Some of the mean girls from school accused me of being pregnant since we were getting married. I wasn't, but with their hurtful words, the arrows lodged again. We were nineteen years old and had never had any conversations about marriage, children, money, faith, or goals. We were a couple of kids who thought we had it all figured out and just wanted to be together. Boy, did we have a lot to learn.

Our wedding, 1988

Suddenly, we found ourselves married and living two thousand miles from home, where we had no support system around us. Kentucky was beautiful, with all its gorgeous foliage; it was a part of the country we had never experienced. When I saw the fall leaves for the first time, I was enraptured! I had never seen such vibrant color. I was an assistant manager at a retail store and we developed strong friendships with my boss and her husband. We spent our fun time off-roading with them or hanging out. The boys got themselves stuck in the mud on numerous occasions, sometimes when they were supposed to be somewhere else, like Thanksgiving dinner. Richard was gone a lot on duty in the field, as he was a communications specialist, assigned to a combat engineer unit.

We had fun, we fought, we had fun, we fought, and so on. Neither of us really knew how to do this thing called marriage.

My Husband's Family Comes to Faith

While we were still in Kentucky, Richard's entire family got "saved"; I wondered what that was supposed to mean. We came home to visit, thinking, *Who are these people, and what happened to them?* His older brother, Ron, had been in some serious life-and-death trouble, and his marriage had fallen apart as well.

We found out that my best friend from high school, Kelli, had moved down the street from Richard's parents. She and her boyfriend had come to know Jesus and had invited Him into their hearts; their lives were transformed. This sweet friend of mine happened to be riding her bike in front of my in-laws' house and wiped out. Richard's mom went out to help her and brought her into the house. They knew each other, of course, and began to share their hearts with each other. Richard's mom poured out her heartbreak and fears about her son, and my friend shared the light and hope of Christ. This friend invited Richard's parents to her church that day and they started attending.

Ron was in a desperate and hopeless situation prior to; he had a gun in his mouth, ready to pull the trigger, and cried, "God, if You are real, please show me. Please save me." God showed up powerfully, and he was instantly sober, and an unexplainable peace came over him. He began to go to church and found a personal relationship with Christ. His life was not instantly "fixed," of course; it was a long, slow process, but that was when it started. He had just started going to church and had accepted Christ one week before my friend and my mother-in-law had that conversation.

We did not know or understand the details of all of this until much later. Truth be told, we didn't really want to hear about any of this or God. Richard and I were far from God and certainly did not want to be "preached at."

Pregnancy Scare

Richard had enlisted for three years. As his time in the army drew to a close, he often said that the only way he would reenlist was if his wife got pregnant. Well, sure enough, a couple of missed birth control pills, and bam, I was pregnant. I don't think I ever went a month *without* forgetting one of those pesky little pills but absolutely not on purpose. I was pretty scared about being pregnant. I certainly did not feel I was ready to have a baby. However, despite what he'd said, we talked it over and decided he would not reenlist. We were ready to go home.

One of the unbelievable things about being in the army at that time was that when I went on base for my pregnancy test, I learned they would not call me with the results; they had to call Richard. How absurd! He called me at work to tell me the news. I was speechless … shocked and scared at first.

He said, "Be happy, baby. I'm happy!"

"We need to tell my parents," I said.

"I already called both of our parents before I called you," he said—he was that excited about it. "What?", I cried, "How could you tell them before me?"

On the day before we were to move back home to Arizona, I had a prenatal checkup, and the doctor coldly told me that my hormone levels had dropped; this meant I had lost the baby.

"Wouldn't I have noticed?" I demanded.

Both of us were in shock and disbelief.

There were going-away parties and coming-home parties, and after getting this news, I drank alcohol at every party, and I also had picked up Richard's habit of smoking socially too.

Back in Arizona, Still Pregnant

After moving home, I became very sick and vomited often. I went to the doctor and was quite alarmed to find out that I was still pregnant. I hadn't lost the baby, and I felt this must surely be my miracle baby. We were once again excited, but I worried about how my drinking and smoking for that short time could have affected our baby. It was hard to believe that I was going to be a mom at twenty-one years old.

We moved in with my parents since we had no money or jobs yet. It was hard to move back home after we had been living life our own way, to come back under their rules. First, Richard worked door to door, trying to sell water purification systems; then he was part of a union painting crew. After that, Richard started working for the owner of a small demolition company; he started on the shovel.

After three months, we borrowed money from his parents for a down payment on a condo. Richard worked around the clock, double and triple shifts. He sometimes slept in his truck to pick up extra shifts, just to keep food on the table. We were often digging through our coin jars, trying find enough money to make ends meet.

With the stress of everything going on, we started fighting. We fought about everything—money, bills, Richard working so much, etc. We did not have good communication skills back then, not enough tools in our toolbox for dealing with conflict. On top of that, I was experiencing a complicated pregnancy. I had a job at a local bank and kept working, even though I had to stay seated all the time and leave early. Life was tough, including financially.

Our first daughter, Alicia, was born—such a beautiful baby and so tiny, only six pounds. My husband was overjoyed; love gushed from him. It's hard to describe what you see in a daddy's eyes when he first holds his newborn baby. The love and wonder filling Richard's brown eyes stirred my heart deeply. He had to be Alicia's main caregiver at first because I was recovering from a C-section, and it was a tough and painful recovery. This brought us closer, for a time.

Adjusting to the routine of a new baby can be rough, especially the sleep routine. It was incredibly hard to get her to sleep, which took a huge physical and mental toll on us. We would often drive her around until she went to sleep; then we'd hope to get her back inside and into her crib without waking her up. We rarely were successful. I had to go back to work at the bank after six weeks, which was terribly difficult, as my body definitely was not ready. I was exhausted and still had lots of healing to do, but we had no choice—or so we thought. We needed the money.

Where Was Our Faith?

Whenever we visited Richard's family, we could not deny the unbelievable transformation in the lives of every single one of them. Even his dad's heart had softened and was filled with Christ's love. I understand it now, from the inside, but neither of us could see it then. We still wanted nothing to do with it. We told them not to talk to us about God; we didn't want to hear it. Our hearts were hardened for sure.

I didn't grow up going to church and had no experience with what was happening with my in-laws. My mom's family was Catholic, but at some point, she became jaded and walked away, seeking her own faith journey. So many people have been hurt in and through the church, globally. When a church gets caught up in legalism, man-made rules, and judgment of others, in any denomination, people are hurt and disillusioned, and they walk away.

We occasionally attended church on Easter and Christmas, but I never saw any interest from my dad. Mom always has been a seeker, a very spiritual person who loved exploring faith ideas and spiritual options. I would describe her beliefs at that time as a combination of Christianity, Eastern religion, and New Age elements, all rolled up together. (She might explain it differently, and that is OK; I'm not judging her. I only love her.) This is all background information to help explain my intermingled beliefs at that time. It is true that whatever our parents believe influences what we believe until we reach an age when we need to seek and decide for ourselves.

While I was very resistant to hear what my husband's parents had to say about their new found faith, I respected that they didn't push it on us or preach to us. They still don't. They just lived it, walked it, and loved us unconditionally. They made it known that they were always there if we needed them.

In fact, throughout our marriage, they were great about not giving us unsolicited advice. They never have meddled in our marriage or parenting. I always have respected them for that, and it has served as a lesson for us in dealing with our own adult children. We now know just how hard it is to turn off the parenting when they move out that door. Help me, Lord!

References

1. 1. Dave Willis. AZQuotes.com, Wind and Fly LTD, 2021. https://www.azquotes.com/quote/1351452, accessed August 31, 2021.
2. *Adam Bede,* George Eliot (1859), chapter 54

3

My World Fell Apart

To love at all is to be vulnerable. Love anything, and your
heart will certainly be wrung and possibly broken.
—C.S. Lewis

Over time, Richard and I continued to drift apart. We were still drinking, but with a baby to care for, alcohol became less appealing to me; Richard, though, was still eagerly indulging. At age twenty-two, we were married and had a baby, but what did we really know about each other? Things were tough intimately too. It often was difficult for me because of all the physical and emotional damage I had experienced, not to mention the financial stress and him being overworked. We had tried counseling in Kentucky, but it hadn't helped much. Things got worse and worse until one day, after we had been fighting, he told me he was moving out.

My whole world turned upside down in that instant. Things seemed to move in slow motion as I spun. I was stunned—how could this be? What I feared most had just happened. I was being abandoned, left alone, just as I had always feared. My heart was scorched. The rug was ripped out from under me. I could not function; I could not go on.

As Richard was walking out the door, I knew exactly where I needed to go—straight to his parents. I wanted to tell them to take me to church because I just couldn't do this on my own anymore. I was so sick—I could hardly walk, couldn't eat, couldn't keep anything down, and was losing weight daily. His parents wrapped me in their loving arms and brought me to church. It was then my eyes were opened. I could hear Christ's call, His love enveloping me. Into Him, I fell—finally believing, inviting Him in, asking Jesus to be my Lord and Savior.

"I cannot do this on my own. Please help me!" I cried. He came alongside, spoke to me through His Word, and came to me in dreams and visions and through songs. Through the counsel of wise and godly people, I learned that whether or not my husband and I reconciled, I would survive. I would be OK.

Christ was within me, healing my heart, transforming me from the inside out, slowly. I began to learn about prayer and the power of it. I was on my knees, fervently praying for my husband's heart to be opened, for conviction, for the blinders to be removed from his eyes and ears, for reconciliation. I had a rock of support around me—so many prayers, and so many shoulders. We are not meant to do life alone but in community. Leaning on others in times of trouble and then, in turn, being there for others when they are in need is what it's all about.

The Bible tells us to love God with all our heart, all our soul, all our mind, and all our strength and to love our neighbors as ourselves.

I began to find my strength, my courage, my power in God—an unexplainable peace amid the tragedy. How can I explain what it is like to finally believe—to surrender, to let the walls come crashing down, and to invite Christ in and believe He is who He says He is: Lord of Lords, God's only Son, sent here to reconcile us to the Father? He redeems us, pays our penalty upon the cross, washes us in forgiveness, heals our broken hearts, and cleanses us as white as snow.

Finally, I Could See

How can I possibly describe what happened inside me, transforming me from the inside out, a filling of peace and joy I cannot contain? It's like trying to describe the beauty and colors and vividness of a glorious sunset to someone who is blind. Unless you have experienced this yourself, you cannot fully comprehend what happens in your soul. It is a filling up, a filling of a hole, a God-shaped hole only He can fill, one designed just for Him. You know it, you feel it, and you sense it. You feel Jesus, hear Jesus, and know Jesus. It is not just blind faith but an in-dwelling of the Holy Spirit that *enables* you to see and to understand, even if you cannot put words to it.

Richard would come home to spend time with Alicia; he did love her deeply. I wondered how could he do that and then walk away again.

He was lost and broken and confused himself. I'm not making excuses or condoning his behavior, just speaking truth. He had his fair share of brokenness in his childhood too. Some difficult and painful things shaped and damaged him as well, but that is his story to tell.

He had shut off everyone, not just me. He cut off his parents, his brothers, his friends—everyone who tried to talk reason with him. Finally, he let his older brother in. Ron spent some time talking to him, sharing from his own experience, as he had been through a terrible and painful divorce.

We were apart for a couple of months, but God broke through, convicting Richard's heart. One day, Richard came to me, broken and humbled and remorseful. He asked me to take him back; he wanted to make our marriage work. He seemed extremely sincere. I was cautious, of course, and we moved very slowly, but I knew in my soul that we were meant to be together. I could see, deep within him, the man I knew was in there. God revealed to my spirit the good man, the great man buried deep inside that even Richard could not see.

I thought the miracle would be in his returning and truly wanting to make things right—and it was. Being together after, however, was more painful and difficult than I could have ever imagined. The hurts ran deep, and I felt the lack of trust was nearly impossible to overcome. Rebuilding a relationship takes time—*much* more time than you might think or than you ever want it to be. In perseverance *you choose to do it God's way*. We went to counseling and a Catholic Marriage Encounter weekend. Though we were not Catholic, this helped immensely. We were challenged with each breakout session to write letters to each other, creating deep and painful conversations on a level we had never had before. I continued to be intensely in church, praying for our marriage and his soul constantly. Eventually, Richard started to come with me to church, and over time, God got hold of his heart. Richard invited Christ in and was baptized. I was overjoyed—another miracle.

Healing Began

Our relationship began to heal, and we grew together, loving and supporting one another. I became a pillar of prayer and faith. For many years, however, I was the rock of our faith, the spiritual leader of our home, always praying for God to get hold of Richard's heart in this way. Praying that Richard would step into the God-designed role of husband and father. However, he would slide away too easily and too often.

Later, we decided to have another baby and buy our first home. What an exciting time for us but scary too. I broke out in hives upon signing the papers for the house. Before long, we welcomed another beautiful daughter, Amanda, into this world. Motherhood is such a gift; you grow and are stretched in unimaginable ways and are filled with new kinds of love that cannot be adequately described. I loved watching my husband play with our daughters, and I still do. Perhaps because he was the baby of his family, he was and is always so playful, full of laughter, jokes, and silliness. Sometimes, I envied that in him; I always was so serious. How much of that was a product of my brokenness, and how much was due to my being the older child? It seems like the oldest children in many families tend to strive for perfection, trying to do everything "right". They are the responsible ones. Yet there were other times when I wished Richard would take things more seriously and quit joking around all the time.

Opposites really do attract, but the things that attract you in the beginning often annoy you after a while. But this is by God's divine design. We each have our strengths and weaknesses; each is meant to complement the other. Where I am weak, He is strong; where He is weak, I am strong. It's about recognizing the God-given strengths and gifts in your spouse, working together, and—just as important—giving them grace in their weaknesses. And isn't that what we want also—grace instead of criticism and judgment over our own shortcomings? We know what those shortcomings are, don't we? We don't need them thrown in our faces.

It has taken Richard and me a long time to see this, to realize we truly are different by design and for a purpose, and to truly value each other's differences.

> Healthy, mutually supportive marriages are no accident. To build a vibrant marriage, spouses need to understand and value each other's strengths, and then draw on those differences to build meaningful oneness. God has designed our differences to complete not defeat us. (Cox 2009)

We had a pretty great yet stressful life for a while. Over time, we moved again, into a larger two-story home. We worked hard, played hard, went on many trips, and spent lots of time with family. Both of us are so very thankful to have close-knit families who really love each other and stand by each other. Our family also became close friends with another family just down the street. Our kids grew up together. We have a beautiful history of doing life with each other.

Our Company Was Birthed

Richard continued to exceed expectations and excel in the demolition company for which he worked, climbing the ladder higher and higher. He had so much drive and ambition and an incredible work ethic, passed down from his father and, in turn, to our children as well. Richard became a lead man, then foreman, then project manager, estimator, and then vice president. With each promotion came more money and a higher standard of living, more spending, more playing, as well as busier schedules, longer hours, and more stress. We would blow off steam by drinking on the weekends in social settings, although not usually at home. Unfortunately, Richard did not see eye to eye with his boss, and, finally, Richard could take it no longer.

I was working my way up through the ranks at The Vanguard Group, an investment company, managing a staff of Client Service and Investor Information associates. Before long, I was promoted to start a Problem Resolution Department in the Arizona call center. At one point, I was sent to San Francisco for a conference, and Richard came also. While there, he and I met with my aunt and uncle, Nancy and Colin, for dinner. My uncle was a senior partner for Accenture, overseeing the western half of the United States. My aunt was an extremely accomplished and respected businesswoman, managing IT for a large law firm.

Richard shared his struggles at work and his decision to leave. He explained he had two job offers and was taking this trip to decide. My uncle started with a barrage of questions about profit margins and the type of work—what work was out there? He started running through numbers on cocktail napkins. He threw out a question: "Why don't you start your own business?"

"There is no way," Richard said. "We don't have the money."

After more questions and conversation, my uncle said, "Present us with a business plan that we can agree to, and the money is yours." They would be an investment partner and backer.

We about fell out of our chairs! Had we heard that right? We didn't sleep at all that night.

Back at home, we went to the bookstore—this was before the internet—to find books on how to write a business plan, how to do projections, and so on. Richard quit his job, and we officially started our demolition company. It was scary for us, yet exciting too. My husband instantly had work and a crew, as he had such a solid reputation in the industry. We started out of our home and garage, with me doing the books by night. My other aunt and uncle, Janet and Chuck, were instrumental in this process as well. They were so supportive and offered great advice. Janet was a CPA and taught me much about accounting and setting up our books, as I had no clue at the time. Chuck gave Richard the courage and the push to actually quit his job and step into this challenging offer.

We worked around the clock, with Richard bidding and selling, project managing, and even make collection calls from atop a backhoe. I worked at Vanguard by day and did the books by night for at least a year. The girls were young, in early grade school. I don't know how we ever survived those exhausting days. I still have many regrets about being *so* busy when my kids were little and not spending nearly enough time with them. I wish I could go back and change that. We have two adult daughters now, both beautiful, inside and out. They are hardworking, talented, compassionate, and funny (they still keep that silly little girl inside; I love it). They both have great heads on their shoulders, and we are extremely proud of them. They tell me all the time to stop beating myself up about my parenting; they turned out fine. We love that we have such a close relationship with them now, even though there were years that certainly were rough.

Early after starting the business, we ran out of money. We couldn't believe we ran out so fast. With great fear, we called Colin and Nancy.

He asked, "Is the work there? Is it profitable?"

"Yes, it is," Richard replied.

"Then go after it. Revise your projections, and show me what you need."

Year after year, we exceeded our projections and expectations.

I must say what an incredible gift they gave us, enabling us to create this kind of wealth and livelihood for our family. Both sets of aunts and uncles contributed to this legacy-building, and we are deeply grateful. Colin and Nancy, who invested in us, strongly believe in helping family members in funding education and entrepreneurship. They have backed many to start their businesses. What difference-makers they are, truly giving back.

After a year, we decided to move out into office space and to hire more staff but also for me to quit my job and come on board full time as office manager and controller. That was another scary decision, as I carried all the benefits. Our company had grown and become more successful each year. We were able to weather a severe downturn in the economy by being conservative and smart in our money management.

Where Was Our Faith?

We became consumed with work and affluence, trips, parties, spending, and activities in which God was being pushed out. We were going to a great church but we went only when it was convenient, or when we felt like it, or when we were in town. We believed, but we lived for ourselves. Our girls were very engaged in the great kids' programs there, and that had us going more often for a while. They were involved in church camps and youth groups. Somehow, we were living with one foot in and one foot out. We went to church but did our own thing the rest of the time. We were not committed in our faith, our time, our service, or our money.

It's no wonder that years later, after our girls left for college, they both walked away from the Lord. My heart breaks, both have commented on how hypocritical Christians can be and that is part of why they left faith. That's just what we were, yet we couldn't see it. If we had been in as strong a place of faith then as we are today—closely walking in the Lord and not being a poor example—I wonder if our girls would have walked away? Yet I must not be filled with guilt. Each person must choose which path to walk. How long did it take for Richard and I to finally get it, to finally walk in this beautiful place? We all have to find faith for ourselves—not what our parents believe but our own faith and relationships.

References

1. Cox, Rodney. 2009. *Different by Design Small Group Study: Discovering Uniqueness—Developing Unity.* Ministry Insights International, Inc.
2. *The Four Loves* by CS Lewis © copyright CS Lewis Pte Ltd 1960. Reprinted with permission.

4

THE DIAGNOSIS THAT
ROCKED OUR WORLD

With man this is impossible, but not with God;
all things are possible with God.
—Mark 10:27 (NIV)

Our affluence, stress level, and ability to do anything we wanted drew us away from God, although we didn't see it immediately. It was a subtle process, a slow fade. We decided, once again, that we wanted a bigger, better home and began the building process. During the beginning of the build, our builder went bankrupt. We decided to save money and act as our own general contractor. What a brilliant idea—not! We were working full time in our business, had young children, and now we were attempting to build a house too. Were we out of our minds? My stepdad was a huge help during this process, as we could not be there all the time. Yet we ran into problem after problem—storm damage twice, for example—that had nothing to do with my stepdad. The pressures were mounting; stress and anxiety took over once again.

Around this time, we were trying to secure new life insurance. Our agent asked how long Richard had had liver disease.

"What?" I replied in surprise. "He doesn't."

The agent explained the rating on our previous policy; we had never understood this. I pushed Richard to the doctor immediately to see what was causing his liver enzymes to be elevated. The doctor seemed unconcerned; he just kept checking and saying they were not that elevated. This made me uneasy, I would not accept that answer and found a new doctor.

Richard was not taking it seriously either. He had never been really sick, never had a broken bone, never been hospitalized or even had a cavity.

This new doctor did take it seriously. He ordered an ultrasound, where they found a massive tumor in Richard's liver, bigger than a man's fist.

The biopsy came next. Richard still was not concerned. Then the phone call came while he was driving.

"Hey, can you talk?" his doctor said.

This can't be good, Richard thought. "Yes, I am driving."

"Well, I need you to pull over. I have some news to discuss with you." After Richard indicated he'd pulled over, the doctor said, "The biopsy was positive for liver cancer. I need you to check yourself into the hospital immediately for further testing."

"I can't do that! I have a company to run!" Richard exclaimed.

"I'll give you twenty-four hours to get your affairs in order and get yourself checked in," the doctor said, "or I'll call your wife or whoever else I need to."

Richard came home and told me the diagnosis. He did not tell me, until well after that there was a five percent chance of survival.

Talk about ripping the rug right out from under us and throwing me into a complete tailspin. *How can this be? How can this be happening?* I then had to call our parents and siblings and closest friends and tell them. We had to tell the company; it rocked each of them too. And we had to tell our girls, although not quite the severity of it at the time. They were only eight and eleven.

Richard checked into the hospital, and they ran every test known to man, it seemed; tubes and probes were everywhere. Ultimately, there was great news, in that they found no cancer anywhere else. They sent the biopsies to Emory University for a second opinion, and there, it was confirmed. We were told that the tumor was in the left and right lobes of the liver, and they were not sure if it was operable. Our doctor suggested the best liver surgeon in the state.

Richard was discharged, and we called to schedule an appointment. It was six weeks out.

"Seriously?" I said. "He's dying over here."

They told us, "Everyone who calls us is dying."

Our Agonizing Wait

This was the longest wait of our lives. We seemed to walk around in a trance. This crisis drove me back to my knees in anguish and pleading through prayers. Why is it that in times of trouble, we draw near to God, seeking him, and when things are good, we can tend to fall away? Why do we forget? How heartbreaking this must be to Jesus.

I refused to fail in prayer. I was on my knees constantly, crying out to save and heal my husband. Rooted in faith and belief, I was surrounded by a throng of mighty prayer warriors, all united in fervent prayer. I had been a prayer warrior before; I would do so again. The day of the appointment eventually arrived. The doctor said the surgery would be very tricky, but that he could do it. Of course, this was scheduled many weeks out as well, so again, we had a long wait. Finally, the big day came. The doctor told us the surgery would take many hours. They would cut Richard open and basically remove all his guts to remove the tumor and gallbladder. Then they would recreate and graft a biliary tree and salvage what they could of the liver.

The surgery took a couple of hours longer than expected—a couple of agonizing hours as I paced the waiting room, wearing out the carpet. The doctor came out, looking haggard, and dropped down next to me, slumping in his chair.

"I got it all," he said. "Richard needed blood transfusions, but I got it all. And while we were in there, the tumor was biopsied again—it was negative for cancer. I can't explain it."

Well, I could! Through the power of prayer, a miracle was worked in him. God was not finished with Richard yet. The tumor, even if it were benign, would have killed him had it not been removed and caught just in time. Doctors can remove 70 percent of the liver, and the patient can survive because the liver is the only organ that regenerates. Seventy percent was what the surgeon took from Richard, and his liver, over time, fully regenerated.

Touch and Go

The night after the surgery, Richard almost did not make it. An angel of a nurse let me stay at his side in intensive care throughout the night—they were not supposed to allow that. He burned with fever and had to be packed in ice and she let me help. It was weeks before he was strong enough to be discharged. I slept in my car at the hospital until then. Thankfully, my neighbor and one of my best friends took care of my kids for me though this. What a godsend she was!

Richard was in the hospital for weeks with a tube down his throat forever, it seemed. At one point, they tried to remove it too soon, and he went into distress. His belly blew up larger and larger as he moaned on the bed with his eyes closed. They had him on high levels morphine for a long time. He thought it was a conspiracy to keep him there and that I was in on it. He started ripping out tubes and IVs and the catheter, all of which had to be reinserted.

Finally, he came home. It was a *very* slow recovery; he was extremely weak. It took a full year before he felt like himself again.

This was another big wake-up call for us. God had spared Richard's life, and it was then that I saw that He had big plans for my husband. We decided we needed to get more serious about our faith and to join our weekly church neighborhood Bible study group. We also decided to finally tithe regularly. We were much more serious about going to church and felt closer to each other than ever at that point.

All of this happened in the middle of building our house. Richard was out of work for a while. I was trying to hold down the fort at our company, while handling the house-building issues and responsibilities at home with the girls. What a terribly grueling, exhausting, scary time. When we finally finished our house and moved in, we were eager to put this year behind us.

5

OUR DAUGHTERS

What it's like to be a parent: It's one of the hardest things you'll ever do, but in exchange, it teaches you the meaning of unconditional love.
—Nicholas Sparks

Alicia and Amanda, 1998

After we moved into our new house, we decided to move our kids to a Christian school. We wanted a stronger faith influence for them and, hopefully, a better education. They were in the fourth and seventh grades at the time. My older daughter, Alicia, fought hard against going at first, but after she was there, she fit right in and made friends. We never had to worry too much about her. She didn't get into trouble, got good grades, and always did her homework. She would antagonize her sister, however, the quiet one behind the scenes, coming across as innocent while stirring the pot when no one was looking.

Alicia has always been creative, like me. We have a lot of similarities in personality and looks. We both are more reflective and need to think things through. Both of us are firstborns and tend to be the responsible list makers and rule followers. We love beauty, the outdoors, and the arts. She is bright, beautiful, funny, and independent. School was easy for her, as was making friends. She took a sewing class in seventh grade and loved it. This started a passion for the theater and costuming. Later, she completed an internship at the Arizona Broadway Theater and then went off to college in Los Angeles, graduating from the Fashion Institute of Design and Merchandising.

Los Angeles is a tough place to make it into the entertainment industry and an expensive place to live as well. She gave it a go for a while but then came back to Phoenix to build her skills and save some money. She was hired as the costume shop manager at the Arizona Broadway Theater, where her talent and skills grew. For many years now, she has been back in LA, making her way. Working in the creative fields is a tough way to make a living. Nonetheless, she has been diligent in fighting for her dreams, often sewing around the clock on various side projects.

She is a fighter and incredibly talented and is able to take costumes from design to pattern drafting and draping to construction. She spent quite some time in a supervisory costuming position at Universal Studios and also has had her own costuming business. Now, she creates costumes at a studio for TV shows, movies, and commercials, as a specialty costume fabricator. We are so proud of her and her heart, talent, and perseverance.

Our younger daughter, Amanda, is intelligent, kind, and empathetic. She was and is very smart, but she struggled in school, having trouble focusing and paying attention or sitting still, for that matter. We had to manage her homework and make sure she turned it in. She was diagnosed with ADHD, yet we chose not to medicate but to manage it in other ways. She was a handful, arguing with us regularly; such a strong-willed child. She has always been our talker, she can talk circles around most people.

Richard has shared how much she was like him. They say strong-willed children often end up successful entrepreneurs. This was true of my husband. Amanda had a challenge in making friends back then, like

I did. I watched her in her new school, going down the same road, being bullied and picked on. She told me she sat alone under the gazebo and cried at lunch because no one wanted to have lunch with her. Why are kids so cruel? How could this be happening to my own sweet, beautiful girl, like it did to me? My heart was scorched because I couldn't fix this, and I couldn't stand the thought of her going through what I did. We tried many things, encouraging her to join a sports team or a club or to play musical instruments—ways to meet and interact with new people. Nothing seemed to work. This went on for longer than I care to admit. Finally, after eighth grade, she begged us to go to the public high school, where her old neighborhood friends went. We reluctantly agreed.

It was there, though, that she really blossomed and began to come into her own—a fresh start. Sound familiar? This was even the same high school Richard and I had attended. Later, she went off to college and was remarkably successful. She now has many friends; she is an extrovert and is very involved in swing dancing and the Lindy Hop. She comes alive when she dances, like she was born for it. I watched her come out of her shell through dance. Many new friendships have formed through this passion, along with competing and teaching. What I love most is watching her dancing freely, not caring what anyone else thinks, just having fun. I admit to a little envy here; with all my growth, I am still often too concerned about what I look like to let loose at times, especially when everyone is watching.

Amanda has a culinary degree; her creative talents are most expressed through food. I love when she cooks—what a gift! She decided she didn't want her career to be in a restaurant kitchen, however, and went back for a bachelor's in nutrition. She has worked as a registered diet technician, administering the WIC program (a county program for low-income pregnant women, infants, and children). She has a passion for cooking and helping others with their dietary needs and challenges, along with dancing professionally and teaching.

Amanda has struggled with chronic illness and severe pain for many years now. We have similarities there too, although her struggles differ from mine and have been longer. It is so frustrating to see doctor after doctor, endure so many tests, and have few answers. This can take a toll on anyone, her included, mentally, emotionally, and spiritually. Yet she perseveres, shows great strength, and now is hopeful. One day she will have a mighty testimony of her own.

Funny how different my girls are when they're from the same parents. It just goes to show that we are more than simply the products of our environment and/or upbringing. My daughters look completely different, think and react differently, and have different interests and temperaments. One is quieter and more reflective; the other is louder and more expressive. Yet both are compassionate, smart, hardworking with a strong work ethic, creative, talented, honest, and silly. They still love to play, which thrills me.

While our daughters were in high school, our business continued to grow; in fact, we opened more businesses. I was the controller of them all. The stress was high—we went through Y2K and all its conversions, an IRS audit, a worker's comp audit, and state audit, all around the same time. I was breaking down; the pressure intense. It's hard not to talk shop twenty-four/seven when you and your spouse work together, especially when I could rarely catch Richard at the office, as he was often tied up on job sites. We did work well together, but it took a toll on us. Business ownership is hard and taxing; in ours, the liability was high, yet we've had many rewards as well. Yes, we loved the lifestyle our income provided, but we also were excited about our ability to impact the livelihoods of others in a tangible way. This was an opportunity to give back to the community, to those in need, to the church, and so much more.

Time to Step Out of the Business

With all of these demands and a feeling of not spending enough time with the girls on our hearts, we made the tough decision for me to step out of the business and stay home with them, as well as pursue my art. I missed so much when they were little; now, at least I would be home while they went through high school.

One of the things I love most in this world is the privilege of being mom to these two wonderful girls. Children are such a beautiful gift and a blessing; it feels like your heart will burst. You wonder how you could possibly love more. It also comes with great responsibility, frustration, and heartache. When your children suffer or their hearts are broken, doesn't yours break right along with theirs? Don't you often feel helpless in these situations? It can be truly agonizing. Yet I would not trade all that for the world. I pray that one day they get to experience holding their own children in their arms. The love that abounds is indescribable.

We Are Not Perfect Parents

Many regrets fill my thoughts if I dwell on it too much—all the "woulda, coulda, shoulda" moments. Why didn't I spend more time with my girls when they were little? Why couldn't I have been a better example, been a better mom, been more patient and kinder? I suppose we all go through this to some degree. As I said, there are no perfect parents; I'm certainly not. Listen, if you have little ones, cherish them. The laundry and dishes, messy house, to-do list, and social calendar can wait. Squeeze them a little longer, be silly, play with them, tell stories, play dress-up, laugh and laugh. Because before you know it, they will be gone, and you will be an empty-nester, just like me.

I have regrets, but you know what? There is plenty we did right too. I hold on to that. We were fairly strict because we loved them. We made family dinners and discussions a priority. We always were there for them, no matter what, and they knew it, and still do. We came alongside them and helped them to succeed.

At times, it was (and is) difficult to understand when to help and when to not help because we wanted them to be independent. Yet in those times when they needed help, we wanted to be there for them. We believed it was important to be involved in their lives but not to be helicopter parents, hovering over them. They needed to make their own mistakes and learn from them.

As parents, we often want to protect our kids, to spare them the pain of making the mistakes we did. Yet it is through those times that *we* learned and grew the most. It was no different for them. Some things, they really did have to learn for themselves. They knew we were there, loving them unconditionally, and that meant everything to them.

> You are going to make mistakes; we made mistakes; nobody has a perfect family. Ours was not perfect, your is not perfect. Hang in there, trust God, and do the best you can. (Wilson)

I am reminded that each day is a new day. I can choose differently going forward. We can still be a positive influence in the lives of our adult children, and until the day we die, our job is never done. This does not mean meddling, of course, but being available to spend time with them, encouraging them, and being there when they want to talk or need counsel. There are new challenges in parenting adult children. It's hard to turn off the unsolicited advice, but that is so necessary. Let's face it; they are adults with their own lives to live, not ours. What they do or don't do is not a reflection on us. However they wish to live their lives is their own choice. We can love them and pray for them, be there for them, and have fun with them, but we need to learn to let go and trust them to live their own lives. This is still a work in progress for me, but I am getting there. Yet for serious situations, we may be called to speak the truth in love about our concerns. This is where we need to pray for wisdom and discernment on how God would have us proceed—whether we should speak up or keep our mouths shut, trusting Him for the right words and timing if we do speak.

We tend to blame ourselves when things don't go right with our children, as if it's somehow our fault—we should have led them better, taught them better, and so on. I am encouraged by something I recently read:

> I would like to remind you that you were very young when you were raising your children, and although you worked very hard, you had to grow up alongside them. It isn't really fair to expect yourself to have known what you had no way of knowing, now is it? Please acknowledge that you did the best you were capable of, given the resources available back then. Now relax dear one. Job well done. (Boorn 2013)

Amen. Just what I needed to hear, maybe you too? Time to let go and rest in who and where we are now and where our children are.

I love spending time with my girls, I wish there was more of it these days, but I take advantage of any time I do have with them, in gratitude, cherishing every moment and praying for them every day.

References

1. Boorn, Wendy. 2013. *I Thought I'd Be Done by Now, Volume One: Hope and Help for Mothers of Adult Children Searching for Peace.* Phoenix, AZ: Perfect Bound Marketing.
2. Wilson, Don. Weekly sermon. Christ Church of the Valley, Peoria, AZ.
3. Sparks, Nicholas. 2018. *The Wedding.* New York, NY: Grand Central Publishing.

6

Through the Eye
of the Storm

*Is today a day to gather strength from the storm - a day to
learn life lessons for the next battle? Or is today a day to sit
by the fire and watch the storm rage outside? Either way, the
storm is just life. Give thanks for all of Life.*
—Jonathan Lockwood Huie

Cozumel is one of the premier dive sights in the world, with warm, pristine waters and incredible coral reefs. As advanced certified divers, my husband and I decided to visit with my aunt Janet, uncle Chuck, and another couple who were close friends of ours, Tina and Joella. We arrived on a Saturday in 2005, with plans to leave the following Thursday. Two tank dives were scheduled for Sunday, Monday, and Tuesday. The resort was wonderful, a tropical oasis of palapa roofs, lush palms, and stunning white sand beaches. We decided to plan afternoon diving so that we didn't have to get up early—what a fabulous idea!

The first dive was spectacular. It was a wall dive, where we had channels and swim-throughs in the coral wall. Looking to the left was like looking out into the deep blue abyss. It was absolutely gorgeous; the colors were so vivid and the water crystal clear. I felt like Nemo from the children's movie *Finding Nemo* at the drop-off. I had been on a mission for years to dive with majestic sea turtles, and finally, I was able to enjoy this experience.

After the dive, we decided to get dressed up and hit downtown for dinner and dancing. We had a fabulous dinner. A man who worked there was "messing" with everyone. He had a fake giant cockroach that he would set in front of a woman. Of course, she would scream and jump up; he got them every time. Another of his tricks was to drop something loud and heavy behind someone and get the same reaction. He had many ploys, all hilarious. He pulled up a chair, sat at our table, and pulled out a deck of cards to do some magic tricks for us. He was the best close-up magician we had ever seen; every trick had us stumped. He then proceeded to make outrageous balloon hats for each of us to wear. We were laughing so hard that we were crying! We then took over the dance floor and got the party started!

The next morning, some of us laid out on the beach while the others rented Jet Skis before heading back out on a dive trip. These dives were incredible; one was in shallow water. We drifted over a sandy bottom. We came upon an area where the dive master found a twelve-inch seahorse swaying in the current. As we started to swim away, my friend got my attention and pointed. The seahorse had let go of its coral and was scooching across the sand, back and forth. We were mesmerized. All of us talked about how amazed we were by the gorgeous water and air temperature. We were never too hot, never chilled—the water was in the eighties, which was absolutely perfect. We were diving at ninety feet with no wetsuits and did not have the slightest chill.

Little did we know what was to come.

How Quickly Everything Changed

Later that evening, we heard that a tropical storm had developed into a Category 1 hurricane, but it was not supposed to hit until the weekend. If it came where we were, we would be long gone—we were leaving Thursday morning. It wasn't a concern at that point.

The next morning, Tuesday, we were getting ready for breakfast when my uncle, Chuck, called our room.

"Turn on the news," he said. "The hurricane is now a Category 5 and is headed straight for us."

I was shocked. *This cannot be real*, I thought, but sure enough; we turned on the news and saw the massive hurricane—it was enormous. Reports indicated that it was the fastest-forming hurricane on record, the strongest one to come up through the Yucatan Channel, and the one with the lowest pressure as well. I was stunned, speechless.

At that point, I called Mom—I knew she had to be watching the news—to let her know that my uncle was going to call the airlines to see if we could leave that day. If not, it would be the next day. The news still said that the hurricane would not hit until Friday or Saturday. I could hear the apprehension in my mom's voice; I felt it as well.

We went to breakfast with the rest of our group. My uncle said he'd called the airlines, and they had eight seats available. We all immediately said we'd take them. When he tried to book them, however, it was too late.

We regrouped to discuss the situation. Our original flight was to leave by noon on Thursday. Continental assured us they would fly out. Because the hurricane would not hit until the weekend, the hotel was downplaying the situation.

For us, it was either sit around all day and do nothing or continue with our plans; the van was already rented. We decided to go ahead. Of course, the hurricane was constantly in the backs of our minds, but what else was there to do at that point? We gathered our snorkel gear and any other items for the day.

The island is only fifty-three kilometers long and fifteen kilometers wide, and we were staying on the southwest end, facing the mainland. We decided to head north, toward downtown, as we only had a quarter of a tank of gas. On the way, we stopped at an area for lunch on the water. The sky was partly cloudy, but the clouds were moving pretty fast. It was windy—too windy—and the surf was too high for me to want to snorkel. The last thing I wanted was to pull saltwater up my snorkel. Everyone felt the same way. While I was nervous, I also felt confident that we would be able to leave in time. As we pulled into town, we saw that gas lines were a mile long—outrageous—so we decided to get gas on the way back. I don't know why we thought that would be better.

We then headed across to the windward side of the island and looked out in amazement at the surf. Wave after wave was rolling in—about six- to eight-foot waves. We were surprised they were so big already. The horizon line was not straight, as it always seemed to be. We could see waves rolling in and breaking out there as well. I became more and more anxious.

I was very concerned, as the island was only about fifteen feet above sea level at its highest point. I had watched so much coverage for the recent Katrina and Rita hurricanes, and both of them had a twenty-foot storm surge following the eye of the storm. We'd be done if that hit while we were on this island. I began to pray that we would all be brought home safely to our families. I also prayed that we would make the right decisions when faced with this danger. I seemed more concerned than the others, except for maybe my aunt; she was pretty quiet.

We decided to go a little farther to a place called Coconuts. We saw where the edges of the road were washed out from the previous hurricane. We also saw how close the water was getting to the road even then. Coconuts was up a rocky outcropping with stairs. It probably was the highest point on the island. From there, we could see black clouds moving in our direction, and the wind was really picking up. As we looked out to sea, we saw a solid wall of rain headed straight for us. That was our cue to hightail it out of there; that really rattled me. The rain hit us as we headed down the stairs, and we piled into the van and started down the road. I just wanted to be back at the hotel. I did not want to get caught on this side of the island, unable to pass down the road.

As we made the turn west and headed back across the island toward town, we got ahead of the rain. We were driving on fumes at that point; the needle was on empty. As we entered town, we saw the gas lines were even longer. The choice was to wait in a line and know we would run out of gas, or make a run for it to the hotel and pray we had enough to make it back. We opted for the latter. We just wanted to be back there to relative safety. As we were getting close to the hotel, the van stalled. It restarted, thank God, but we stalled three more times as we pulled into the parking lot of the hotel. We ran out of gas—but in our parking lot. Thank God for small blessings.

They Had No Plan

At the hotel, management said there was to be a 6:00 p.m. hurricane meeting. Many guests were checking out in the lobby and heading for the ferry to go to the mainland. We were told the regular ferry schedule ended at 5:00 p.m.; it was 4:00 p.m. at that point. For many, it was obvious that nerves were running high.

My aunt and I went into the internet room to send a few emails to family and to check the weather forecast and the airlines. Our airline still said the flight was on. There was no change in the weather; still a Category 5 hurricane headed straight for us, set to hit Friday or Saturday. We went to put our things back in the rooms and to pack our bags, just in case we had to make a hasty departure.

Our friends spoke to a pilot who said he absolutely would fly out. He said you could take off in up to Category 2 winds, which the outer bands would be. Plus, our friends said, "Look at the water; it's completely calm."

I turned around to look, and that sent a chill straight up my spine. Not even a ripple; it was like glass—with an eerie glow. This alarmed me more—the calm before the storm, especially since we had seen high surf and strong gusts earlier. I kept questioning myself; I hoped we hadn't made a mistake in not getting on the ferry. I also wondered if the rest of the group realized how serious and deadly a Category 5 hurricane was. I did because I had extensively watched the news during the previous ones.

We went into the theater for the meeting. The manager explained that the storm was heading straight for us. He said if we want to leave, the ferry would run until 10:00 p.m. He kept saying that there were more options on the mainland than on Cozumel, where there was only one flight per day. When specifically asked, he admitted that the hotel was not designed to withstand winds from Categories 4 and 5. The manager said those who stayed would be evacuated to a small shelter downtown at the appropriate time.

Then, an employee ran up and whispered something in the manager's ear.

"The shelters are full," he told us, "so we will stay here"—after he had said it was unsafe. "We will move to the second-floor rooms, farthest from the water."

This hotel was only a few feet above sea level. We also had heard earlier that we were on the low end of the island that was prone to flooding.

At this point, our group met outside and anxiously agreed we were getting out of there. The choice was to leave via ferry and know we would have to hunker down and weather the hurricane, or stay and bet on our flight leaving in the morning, as we were assured it would.

We decided to leave. I believe that at this point, they should have had mandatory evacuation of the island. Praise God that we chose to evacuate when we did.

We grabbed our bags, checked out, and piled into a van in no time. At that point, we saw Kathy, our dive buddy, traveling alone. She seemed distressed and asked if she could go with us. I had seen another couple in the lobby, very distressed, and they became part of our group as well. We were able to get tickets for the 8:00 p.m. ferry.

While waiting for the ferry, we also met up with another dive buddy, Aaron. He joined the group, which brought our number to ten. The ocean was certainly not calm anymore; the swells were rising. The wind was picking up, and rain sprinkled off and on.

At 8:30, there was still no sign of the ferry. Finally, it appeared, off in the distance, slowly rocking toward us. When it pulled up alongside the dock, the crew had a hard time tying it off, as the swells were getting so large.

The rain started coming down in earnest. Almost all the ferry passengers were locals; there were very few tourists then. I guess those who were going to leave already had gone.

The ride was awful. The ferry rocked immensely. Swells caused it to rock ten-plus feet in the air. My IBS flared up, as it often does with stress. (Go figure; no stress here!) The ferry ride took about forty-five minutes. As we neared the shore, I couldn't watch the horizon; the lights would come into the window and then go out of the window and then back again. My stomach lurched violently. I was so thankful that my kids were not with me.

We arrived in Playa del Carmen around 9:15 p.m. As we walked up the street, we saw the windows being boarded up; this was extremely disturbing. Some people were having drinks in Señor Frog's as we passed. We later heard the place was completely destroyed and that water had come in up to the third floor of the hotel.

As we walked up the ramp, I grabbed a taxi driver and told him that we needed to get to the safest hotel in Cancun. There were ten of us, and we needed to find a safe place to weather the storm. He recommended the Radisson Hacienda in downtown Cancun and arranged for taxis to accommodate us all.

It was a forty-five-minute drive to the hotel. In the meantime, Tina was on the phone with her assistant back home. She told him where we were being sent and asked him to try to get us rooms. We were amazed that her phone worked, as none of our phones had service. It was a godsend that her phone worked, as her assistant updated us and tried to keep us one step ahead of the game. Just before arrival, she confirmed that he had secured us rooms. He also tried to move our flight from Cozumel to Cancun as the next possible available option.

I asked the driver, "How far is this hotel from the water?"

"A mile or two," he said.

"How far is it above sea level?"

"About thirty 30 feet," he said.

This reassured me immensely, as the storm surge was my biggest concern. We arrived at the hotel and called our families to let them know we had made it safely. It was hard for me to eat; my stomach was tied up in knots. I prayed for a long time that night. I was thankful that we had made it off the island and to this hotel. I continued to pray for God to keep us all safe and together and to bring us back into the arms of our loved ones. While I knew God would protect us—I had no doubt—I still did not sleep that night.

On Thursday morning, we went down to breakfast and learned our Cozumel flight had been canceled. We would have been trapped, had we stayed. We received word that my friend's assistant had found us flights out of Cancun for that day; we were shocked. We would skate out of there just in time! Talk about the highs and lows of emotions; what a roller coaster. We were relieved and celebrated.

This excitement did not last long. Shortly afterward, he said that airlines were canceling flights left and right out of Cancun. As feared, our flight was canceled. Flights were rescheduled for Saturday now. Each of us went to the gift shop and loaded up on water and all the snacks we could get—peanut-butter crackers, peanuts, chips, cookies.

Impact Imminent

We saw a newspaper in the dining room the next morning with a headline: *Impacto Inminente*. We didn't have to speak Spanish to know what that meant. The *Miami Herald*'s headline was "Colossus Threatens Cancun, Florida." The papers said it was to be the most intense Atlantic hurricane ever. The wind speeds were currently 160 miles per hour. About thirty-three thousand tourists had mandatory evacuation from the hotel zone of Cancun—a strip of land between the lagoon and the ocean, where many of the tourist hotels are. The hurricane was still headed for us. At that point, it was estimated to hit between 2:00 and 3:00 a.m. on Friday.

I found the hotel manager and asked him about the hotel.

"The government has designated it a hurricane-safe hotel," he said. "Later today, guests from two more hotels from the hotel zone will come to this one as a shelter. These people will sleep on the floors, in the ballroom, meeting rooms, and lobby."

We were so blessed to have rooms to sleep in; we had received some of the last rooms available. Many people had it much worse than we did.

Some of our group wanted to find an ATM and additional food. We heard there was a store around the corner that was open until 2:00 p.m., they were closing early due to the impending hurricane coming. We knew that we would be cooped up for a long time, so we decided to go walk until we were forced to stay inside. It was windy, and the clouds moved quickly. Finding the store, we grabbed some more food and some cash. Richard and I had so much snack food in our room that we didn't think it was necessary to get anything more substantial. In hindsight, that was a mistake. Some people purchased bread and peanut butter and tuna fish—a much smarter idea.

Most places were boarding up; it was an indescribably eerie scene, with locals scurrying to and fro. Tensions were running high. The wind was picking up at that point. Truth be told, I was incredibly nervous but decided to stay out a little longer because we were so close to the hotel.

Winds were maybe twenty to thirty miles per hour, with on-and-off rain sprinkles. When we returned to the hotel, the news stations were out. We only received information from the internet, calls home, and Tina's connection. The latest news was that the hurricane had dropped to a strong Category 4 (as was Katrina when it hit), and the eye was headed straight for us. That afternoon, there was nothing to do but wait. We went out front a few times to see what it looked like. The hotel was mobbed, as all the other people were there now from the evacuated hotels. Rain was spitting off and on, and wind gusts were forty to fifty miles per hour as we stood outside watching the storm approach.

Tina and I went up to the fourth floor to try to get an update online, as that is where the guest computers were to get online. As soon as we got on the computer, the power shut off for a few seconds. It was pitch-dark but then it came back on. That certainly gave me a rush of adrenaline and put my heart into my throat. We found no new information and went straight to our rooms to get our dive flashlights. Thank God for them and the extra batteries. I won't travel without a flashlight again.

We grew much more serious about the situation at that point, yet we stayed together a little while longer before heading for the rooms. Now the reports said that the hurricane might not hit until 5:00 a.m. We thought we would try to get a little rest. As usual, I prayed myself to sleep, crying out for God to protect us all. My sleep was restless and sporadic, if you could call it sleep at all. Around midnight, we lost the main power and heard the generators kick on. It then began to rain—and it continued to rain steadily all night long. Wind gusts were still around forty to fifty miles per hour.

On Friday morning, we awoke to solid rain coming down; not a lot had changed. The latest news was that the hurricane would not hit until 5:00 p.m. now. In addition, our flights had been pushed to Wednesday or Thursday. We all called family as often as we could to reassure them that we were safe. My mom became the contact person for us, as she had our girls. It was good to talk to them; I missed them very much. They were all scared, but we explained we had made it to the safest hotel; it was a hurricane rated safe hotel.

Our group went to breakfast and found all the windows boarded up in the dining room. The doors and windows were either boarded or taped in the lobby. We were now locked in; it was strange to eat breakfast, knowing that. As we walked around, we saw people sleeping on the floors on towels. We heard these evacuees had not been allowed to bring any belongings. They had the clothes on their backs and one small pillow each. There were children and elderly on the floors as well; it was instantly sobering. The hotel still provided hot meals for us. Those who had rooms were charged fifteen dollars per meal per person; those who didn't have rooms had to pay cash, if they had it.

I will never again give my husband a hard time about taking too much cash. He always feels better with cash on him. Thank God he did because that cash gave us shelter and food throughout the ordeal. The people who had to evacuate quickly had only the cash in their pockets. All credit cards had stopped working; it didn't matter how much money you had in the bank or on available credit if you could not get to it. We continued to give thanks and praise for being so fortunate to have gotten off the island when we did and for having a bed to sleep in and food to eat.

About noon, the hotel staff called the first hurricane meeting. The manager explained the storm track and said it was to hit later in the evening. From 3:00 p.m. on that day until 10:00 a.m. the next day, we would be confined to our rooms. We were told the safest place was in the bathrooms. He named the room numbers of those most at risk and said those people definitely should stay in the bathrooms. We were not included in that group; they were mostly upper-floor rooms. Remember that there was no electricity. This meant whole families were locked in the bathroom, all night, in the dark. Some were able to get flashlights or buy the few candles that the gift shop had left. Fortunately, we divers had flashlights. We were told to expect to hear glass breaking and debris flying but that this hotel was structurally designed to withstand these winds. The hotel representative told us lunch would be served but no dinner. Provided it was safe, we would have a cold breakfast in the morning.

The weather was much the same until the lock-in period; then it really wound up. I would guess the winds were gusting at seventy to ninety miles per hour and were starting to howl loudly, but with very little rain, surprisingly. We stayed in our rooms for hours, talking, reading the same magazines over and over, waiting, and feeling restless. Richard and I went next door to Tina and Joella's room. We found the others in there, playing cards by flashlight. A couple who had joined our group told us their room was already leaking badly through the bathroom ceiling.

While the wind was howling, it seemed to stay at the same high level for a long time, not increasing. I had a hard time at this point, not sure where I should be. My aunt and uncle were still in our room. Should we be staying there and preparing to get in the bathroom? On the other hand, it was unsettling to wait and wait. Would it be easier next door, playing cards to pass the time? I needed a distraction. Chuck and Jan knew they could come over if they wished. I did feel a little guilty in leaving them. I concluded, much later, that it was more about my needing to know where everyone was and how they were doing at all times.

As Jan put it later, I am a "herder," a mother hen, like my mother before me. I need to keep tabs on everyone and make sure they are OK. It's the mama bear in me.

We did feel safe in the rooms at the time. Once again, I praised God for bringing us to what appeared to be the safest rooms in the hotel. They were on the first floor, and opened into a protected inner courtyard. There were also large columns that partially wrapped our arcadia doors, offering additional protection. This view into the courtyard was all we could see of the storm.

We had heard that we should pressurize the room, so we opened the glass doors several inches. This amplified the sound of the howling. The hallway that the front door faced out to was solid concrete and protected. It was open at the right end so rain and wind blew through. Our friends' arcadia door (sliding glass door) was flapping like it wanted to take off; it seemed to not be secured entirely at the bottom. They wedged furniture between the door and the outer railing to secure it.

The winds rose, and we started to hear glass shattering and debris flying. There were loud crashes nearby that were extremely disturbing. I watched our group play cards that night, as I was too wound up to participate. I was not sure what to do with myself. As the storm worsened, we finally retired to our rooms.

My husband and I lay in bed in the dark, listening to the wind scream into the night. The sound of a freight train is commonly used to describe the wind, but it seemed much more violent and deafening than that. The windows shook vigorously. We heard glass breaking regularly at that point. We curled up, spoon-fashion, together and held on through the night. The sound of windows breaking and debris flying became louder and more frequent, and we could hear people screaming in the distance. Some crashes were so loud that I dived out of bed and onto my feet at least three times. I was terrified!

"Maybe we should be in the bathroom after all," I cried to Richard. The experience was horrible and seemed to drag on forever. This was the longest night of my life. Despite my fear and anxiety, I always felt an underlying peace and knew that we were being taken care of the whole way. Regardless of what people say, faith does not mean that there are not moments of great fear and anxiety in a crisis situation. We are human, after all.

The winds were over one hundred miles an hour by then, and the sound was deafening, screaming into the night. We later heard that when the eye moved on shore, the winds were 150 to 160 miles per hour. We were certainly in the height of the hurricane then. Sometime in the wee hours of the morning, we must have dozed off as the winds died down. We awoke to find a mild, light rain and light gusts of wind. We were ecstatic that we had made it through the night—through the hurricane! Finally, it was over.

Was It Over?

We could see into the courtyard and trees and bushes were down, palm trees were stripped, and debris was all over the place. There were twisted and mangled solar panels strewn about like tin cans. Our group tried to climb the stairs, which were exposed to the elements, but staff immediately turned us back and told us to go back to our rooms. We were only in the eye of the hurricane; it was *not* over—and it was not moving either; the storm had stalled.

Our hearts dropped as we headed back to the rooms. Not long afterward, they decided to let us come out for breakfast. The hallways were flooded. Debris and broken glass were strewn everywhere. At the end of one hall, we could see the tennis courts were flooded. The windows to the gym and ballroom were completely blown out—the CNN news crew was broadcasting from there.

The people who had been sleeping in the ballroom had been moved to the hallways, which also flooded, so they then were moved into the dining room. Every time there was a meal, they had to get out of the way so we could eat. As we went into the lobby, we saw that the glass in the small dome in the ceiling had blown out. Most of the lobby was taped off, and the rain was slipping in through these areas. They had a brief meeting to let us know that the water would be kept off except for one hour, three times per day. This would be the same for the generator.

The hotel did an outstanding job of keeping us fed throughout this ordeal. Many of the staff and waiters worked around the clock. We slipped them money when we could to thank them for being there for us. After breakfast, we braved the stairs again to take a look out. As far as we could see was flooding, uprooted trees, signs strewn about. We saw the McDonald's sign mangled, roofs were blown off, communication towers were down—it was an unbelievable sight. The air was heavy and smelled wet and dirty.

Richard and Chuck came up with the idea of filling up trash cans with water from the pool to be able to flush the toilets. Soon after, many others followed our lead. During the one-hour intervals with water, we did try to take a few fast cold showers. We kept hoping Hurricane Wilma would wind up and get on with it so we could get past this. When evening came, she finally started up again. It was going to be another long night.

The rains came, and the winds were back to fifty to seventy miles per hour and stayed like that for an unbelievably long time. We went back to playing cards by flashlight once again.

Then we heard that the hurricane had dropped to a Category 2. This was good news; we just needed it to move now! As we lay in bed, Wilma ramped up in a huge way. *Category 2, my eye*, I thought. The winds became horribly loud, howling and screaming in the courtyard. I could not believe it, but it was *much* louder than the previous night, although there was less breakage. The sound was horrendous. The arcadia doors kept flexing and bowing. I was so unnerved. Later, we learned it had been louder because on the backside of the hurricane, the winds were blowing in the opposite direction and more directly were hitting our side of the building in the courtyard. It was like a giant wind tunnel.

Somehow, Chuck snored loudly through this! Richard laughed in disbelief and picked up a shoe to throw at him, but I wouldn't let him do that. He asked me if *his* snoring was that bad. I told him, "At times, yes." He just laughed and apologized. It was a long night indeed.

Finally, in the wee hours, we again dozed off. We were very grateful the storm had *really* passed this time. We grabbed a cold breakfast from the dining room and brought it back to the rooms. Because people were roaming about and seeing our rooms, we felt it necessary to keep someone there at all times. Our key cards had stopped working, so the only way we could get back in was to leave the arcadia door unlocked and hop the railing from the courtyard. That had been fine before, but now, anyone who saw us knew that they could get into our room that way. Most of those people had been sleeping on floors; they were thoroughly displaced and had no belongings with them. We could easily see where desperation could lead. I prayed that as things deteriorated, the situation at the hotel would not get ugly.

The energy at the next hotel hurricane meeting was much different than the previous time. They said we were running out of food, water, and generator fuel, with only three days of fuel left. The manager felt that food would be on its way shortly and that we would have a meal later. A woman from the Avalon Hotel said they were looking into the possibility of bussing their people to Merida, three hours away, as there were rumors of extensive damage to the airport in Cancun.

In the breakfast line, we talked to many people and heard their stories. We met two young Irish girls who had been staying on the fourth floor. During the worst of the hurricane on Friday night, their arcadia doors and windows were blown out. Their front door was blown off the hinges. All the furniture was blown around—some of it was on the balcony, and the large armoire was thrown onto the bed. The girls, fortunately, were locked in the bathroom. One had bruises on her legs from trying to hold the door shut through the ordeal. The CNN news crew came to their rescue and brought them down to the lobby. They were sleeping on the floor now.

We heard of a woman who had wandered in off the streets, exhausted and covered in urine. She had been taking shelter somewhere with no food or water and had to pee in a bag. Someone took her in and cleaned her up and gave her clothes. Another couple we talked to had come in from a shelter and said, "You have no idea how good you have it. Conditions are just awful." There was no food or water, and it was so bad that they went roaming the streets, looking for something better.

The Situation Worsens

We went back to our rooms and to inventory our sparse remaining food and water. We were very concerned about the announced food, water, and fuel shortages. We could feel the atmosphere shift after this latest news; the mood around us turned dark. Although things had been fairly calm and orderly, we could see how quickly things easily could turn ugly.

Animalistic behavior can emerge when it comes to protecting and feeding your family. Richard also got out the dive knives and put them on for our protection, just in case.

As we waited for the generator time, we went back upstairs to try to get a phone signal, hoping to let our loved ones know we were all right. As we reached the fourth floor, we saw rooms that were completely blown out. Some looked like a bomb had gone off in them. The standing water in front of the hotel was three to four feet deep. Cars were flooded, power poles were down, nearly all the trees were uprooted, and roofs were blown off. Out back, we saw the roof of a store entirely peeled off and partially caved in. We saw a communication tower bent over a building like it was thin wire. As far as we could see, everything had extensive damage.

Feeling agitated and needing something to do, we started cleaning up the courtyard. We knew we would need water, so we first worked to clean up the pool. The guys also helped haul out trees, shrubs, and debris. A number of other evacuees joined in to help. I think everyone felt better that they could contribute in some small way. We also helped to mop the water from the rooms across from us that were flooded and to sweep the water down the hall.

We could hear random gunshots and sirens outside the hotel; we heard that people were trying to get in, as word got out that our hotel had food and water. The government ended up sending armed guards to surround the hotel.

That night, no one played cards by flashlight. With the shortage issues, we all felt it necessary to conserve every resource we had. Two of the rooms across from us were vacant, but the hotel did not put anyone else in them. We found two groups of people and brought them into those rooms to stay. They were extremely grateful.

One Hispanic lady came down the hall, looking for someone named Lucy. She said someone, speaking Spanish, had called their room looking for me. I went down the hall to find out who it was, but I was too late; the woman had hung up. I later learned it was my mother-in-law. In all the turmoil, I had forgotten she spoke Spanish. I wished we did; we all wished that we did. It was so hard to get good information when we did not understand the language. With as often as we were in Mexico, it was completely ridiculous that we did not speak Spanish.

I had not talked to my girls or family for a while and needed to do so. The phones in the rooms were no longer working, so I went to the lobby with a flashlight. I called Mary Jane as my girls were with her now instead of my mom—thank God for both of them. It was indescribably comforting to know that I didn't have to worry about my girls and that they were being well taken care of.

There was a line at the payphone so I could only speak to them for a few minutes. To hear their voices meant the world to me. Although the call was brief, relief flooded over me after sharing we were all OK.

On Monday morning, Tina, who had been our communication lifeline, said when they turned the generators on, she had found a power strip in the internet area that was live. She was able to charge her phone. By 8:30, the generator still was not on. Tina suggested driving to Merida to fly out from there. She had her assistant check to see if we could get flights from Merida and if we could get rooms. She had heard that someone made it over there, although a three- to four-hour bus ride had taken ten hours. Still, they made it and flew out.

My first reaction was a complete lack of interest in driving for ten hours on a bus into the unknown, but her assistant was able to get us flights for that day at 5:30 p.m. Richard, Chuck, and Joella ventured out from the hotel to the bus station, a mile or so away, to see if we could get on a bus. We packed quickly while they were gone. When they came back, we learned that the bus station was mobbed with people who were anxious to get out of the city, and we could not get tickets. They said that, instead, they had arranged for three taxis to take us to Merida. It was at an exorbitant price, but we were desperate at that point and needed to be *out* of Cancun.

I called home quickly to let them know what we were doing. We took all our bags out the back of the hotel to the taxis. We didn't want to risk anyone seeing our bags and what that potentially could cause. Before we left, we found the Irish girls and told them to take over our rooms.

We happily piled into those taxis and took off down the road. We potentially, finally, were going home.

This was our first real look at the devastation, and all of us were stunned. People were roaming everywhere; many looked shell-shocked. There were unbelievably long lines for food and water. We didn't see a single structure that was undamaged; many were completely destroyed. Gas station steel awnings were mangled on the ground like twist-ties. As we drove on, the scene looked increasingly like a war zone. Amazingly, there was the odd palapa roof or two left intact.

Soon after we left the city limits, a number of vehicles and taxis passed us from the other direction, heading back into town. They seemed to be flagging our taxis to turn around. It was frustrating, being unable to understand what they were saying, but it didn't sound good. We became a bit nervous at this point. Our taxis pulled over a few times to discuss which way to go. The drivers said people were telling them that the roads were flooded and impassable.

Richard ran up to the taxi in front of us to see what was going on. Although the road was flooded, the drivers said we could pay fifty dollars to be pulled onto a flatbed truck to cross. We agreed, of course, wanting to get across. About forty-five minutes out of Cancun, we hit stopped traffic. Getting out to investigate, we found the water was now about thigh deep; no cars could get through it. We did see that buses and large trucks were getting through the water. The taxi drivers said we might want to flag a passing trucker to see if we could jump in with them to cross. In the end, we decided it was not a good idea and we should go back to Cancun, as heart-wrenching as that was. Everyone agreed, except for dive buddy, Aaron, traveling with us, who said there was no way he was going back. He jumped in a pickup truck with two locals to make a break for it.

The return taxi ride was quiet. Although we felt we had made great decisions all along, it now appeared we had not. Maybe we were so intent on getting out of there that we were not patient enough. Tensions were high. *You can't think or plan ahead more than about five minutes*, I thought, *as everything changes as soon as you turn around*. One minute. it was one way, and the next, it was the opposite. It was all about how to handle the *now*. Many prayers went up, no doubt. I realized that there was no control; we could only pray about making the right decisions and put the rest in God's hands.

Too often, we try to control everything and everyone around us. This control is an illusion. We can only control the way we react to a situation and have to put our trust in God. This does not necessarily mean that we sit around doing nothing and wait for God to act. We need to do all that we can do and pray for guidance and wisdom in making the right decisions. And sometimes, God does direct us to wait and be still. Wisdom and discernment are crucial.

On the way back, we were surprised to see that the military had blocked the roads to give out bags of food and water to the hundreds of people waiting patiently in line. It was calm and orderly; I was impressed with this response.

We were worried about returning to Cancun, now without rooms and no plan to get out. We decided to have the drivers drop us off at the bus station. The guys had to argue with the taxi drivers, who wanted full fare for the ride, even though they did not get us to our destination. They settled on two hundred dollars per car to bring us right back where we started. We decided that most of us would stay at the bus station with the luggage and look into getting tickets while two went back to the hotel to see about getting our rooms back. We also needed to get to the fourth floor to get a cell phone signal so we could cancel the flights in Merida.

Our pile of bags for nine people was obscene. We were divers and had brought our own gear, so there was double the luggage. It was embarrassing as people eyed our bags; it was not a comfortable feeling. There was a 5:15 p.m. bus, and we purchased tickets. At this point, I went into panic mode. We had an hour until boarding, but six of our nine people were now missing, including Richard! I don't do well when people are separated; I need to know where they are and that they are OK. Now, we had a deadline to make the bus.

Richard showed up first. "The hotel won't let anyone back in," he said. "We went around back, jumped the fence, and went to our old rooms." The Irish girls were shocked to see them back. "We've decided that we can sneak back in, and maybe the women can share a couple of rooms, and the men can sleep outside."

"We got the tickets," I told him. "We need to board soon."

"I don't have my backpack; it's at the hotel."

I stressed out; my anxiety was through the roof. Richard's passport was in his backpack. He ran back to the hotel to find our friends and the others and tell them the news.

Fortunately, everyone got back in time. Richard got in a line for hot dogs, as we had not eaten since early that morning. We boarded the bus and took our seats, greatly relieved, and ate our Sonoran hot dogs ravenously. We were so relieved that we were on the bus and didn't have to find somewhere to stay for the night. I pondered our decisions: although we questioned our decision to leave in the taxis, if we had not, we wouldn't have been on this bus, heading out of town. If we had not been at the bus station, with all of our luggage, right when they added the extra buses, it would not have happened.

As we approached the water crossing again, there was traffic backed up for a great distance. The bus stopped, and the driver climbed out to see what was going on. When the driver climbed back on, he said the military had blocked the road and were not letting anyone pass. Apparently, a bus had gotten lodged in the middle of the water and tipped over. Unbelievably, we were being turned around again! The bus driver said we could try another way, through towns, but it would be extremely long. He also said there was danger in going the other way, as marauders were possible.

Wonderful, I thought. *What next?*

We all became increasingly anxious once again. He drove right back to Cancun. The driver needed approval to go the other way, or he could try again tomorrow.

It was well past dark, and we were looking at the prospect of being dumped on the streets of Cancun with nowhere to go. We would be sitting ducks. The city was deteriorating and growing more unsafe by the minute. It was so quiet on the bus that you could hear a pin drop. All of us were deep in our own thoughts and prayers, trying to process the situation in our own ways. Maybe we could at least sleep in the bus terminal. There was no way we could sneak back into the hotel at night with guards surrounding it. We were truly frightened at this point. Even those of us who had not seemed scared during the hurricane definitely were now. The bus driver said that even if we went the long way, it would be dangerous. I started to go numb as I looked at this situation and what to do about it.

As we pulled into the station, one in our group said, "You'll have to pry me out of my seat. I'm sleeping on the bus." We all felt that way.

A manager got on the bus and said they had decided to go in a ten-bus caravan the long way. It would be safer that way, and the managers would go on the buses with us. This route was south, down past Playa del Carmen, through Tulum, then west and back up to Merida, through a number of small towns. He explained that if we did not feel comfortable with that route, we could get off—and some did.

We were again ecstatic and relieved immensely to hear that we could stay on the bus and take the road. Anything not to sleep on the streets.

A Terrifying Bus Ride

As we took off down the road, the temperature kept dropping on the bus. The driver had the air conditioning so frigid that it must have been fifty degrees or less. We were miserable, as we were in shorts and tank tops. Several times, we asked the driver to turn the temperature up. He refused because that caused the windshield to fog up, and he could not see. We traveled eight hours on a frigid bus. My teeth chattered as I tried rubbing warmth into my arms and legs, squeezing as tight to Richard as I possibly could. We were so numb and delirious that we started cracking corny jokes and laughing uncontrollably at the silliest things. Often, we passed through flooded areas, and one was particularly deep and long. We knew our luggage had to be drenched below us.

After a while, we headed through a dense, dark jungle. The trees towered above us and encroached on the road, which then became even narrower. The bus driver was flying down the road; he took the corners unbelievably fast. Occasionally, we passed oncoming buses. With the speed he was traveling and the narrowness of the road, we were white-knuckled and bug-eyed! It was certainly enough to keep us awake all night.

Shockingly, in this deep jungle, Tina's cell phone worked. What an unbelievable blessing. She was on the phone in the middle of the night, trying to find us somewhere to go once we arrived. She spent most of the hurricane ordeal glued to her phone, acting as our travel agent and rescuer. She was incredible; I don't know what we would have done without her and her assistant. First, her assistant said there were no rooms anywhere; the original place he'd found had given our rooms away. The embassy and the American consulate were working on trying to find rooms for people, but there just weren't any. He then called another bed-and-breakfast—they could take all twelve of us, which now included three new women we'd brought into our group. We'd met while waiting in line to secure bus tickets. One spoke Spanish, which was extremely helpful. Time after time, we experienced such positive proof of being carefully taken care of by God, every step of the way. Circumstances always fell into place to keep us safe and together. I praised God once again for bringing us through.

Safety at Last

Our group arrived in the bus terminal around 4:00 a.m., completely exhausted and emotionally drained, which was to be expected. We secured taxis, and we were on our way yet again. Our group left the main streets and started winding down dark and mysterious alleyways. This made us extremely nervous—what had we gotten ourselves into now? Where were we going?

We came upon a long, tall wall with a single locked door in it. All I wanted was a shower, a clean warm bed, and electricity. As the door opened, a woman—we learned her name was Bonnie—stood there, welcoming us in. A sanctuary existed inside those walls, a haven like no other. It was dark, but we could see immense grounds, lush plantings, and a beautiful house with detached buildings. We could not help but feel an overwhelming peace when we stepped inside. We all seemed like zombies at that point; we had been trying to get out of Cancun for eighteen hours.

Bonnie showed us to our rooms. I had the best shower I have ever had; peeling away my filthy clothes and letting the hot water wash over my ailing body was divine. Funny how many things you take for granted in everyday life. How long had it been since I'd had a hot shower? How long since I had been able to flip a light switch and have it work. I immediately crawled into bed but, surprisingly, didn't sleep well. I don't think I had slept soundly since we left Cozumel over a week ago.

What a fabulously beautiful feeling to wake to the domestic sounds of a lawnmower next door, the smell of fresh cut grass, and people laughing over a hot breakfast. The grounds were gorgeous, with lush tropical plants and a pristine pool with a large palapa and fountains. Everyone else was already up; I was the last to enter the kitchen. This was when I met Pat, Bonnie's business partner and friend. She made us all mouthwatering omelets for breakfast. It was then that we learned the story of how we were able to stay there.

Their bed-and-breakfast was open only from November through April each year. It was late October now, and Bonnie had recently arrived from Canada. The phone line they used for internet connection was not working, so they had unplugged the connection and plugged it into the main phone line. This blocked any calls from coming in. Therefore, they were unaware of the embassy and consulate trying to reach them for rooms. Right when they unplugged the internet connection, Tina's assistant's call came through—truly a miracle. This is why no one was staying there, and they were able to take us all. If that wasn't amazing enough, we later found out that after *that* phone call, and we had arrived safely and called home to let our families know we made it, that phone line never worked again for the entire duration of our stay there. To add to this, we learned the name of this haven was In Ka'an, which means My Heaven. I couldn't believe it; I just wanted to cry right then. A few stray tears escaped from my eyes, rolling down my cheeks. If that was not divine intervention, then I don't know what is! Every one of us recognized it for what it was and sent up much praise and gratitude.

When I talked to my mom to let her know we had made it there safely and what a sanctuary it was, she confessed that it had been the scariest night for my family and friends as well. We had called from the bus terminal in Cancun after being turned around the second time and told them we were leaving on a ten-hour journey through the jungle at night. Apparently, all were frightened for us on that night and spent hours in serious prayer.

As I mentioned, we arrived at the bus terminal at about four o'clock in the morning. It was at this exact time that Mom received a phone call—the phone rang once and stopped. She felt she was being given the message that we had made it safely. I was relieved to talk to her. We also spoke to my in-laws, my dad, and my daughters. What a relief—we were finally out of danger.

It was Tuesday, and we had flights out on Friday. Our group decided to head into town to explore. Merida was a picturesque colonial city; we were amazed with the beauty and architecture surrounding us with its plazas and beautiful cathedrals. Narrow streets were filled with colorful facades in peach, periwinkle, and shades of green. We thought we had seen a lot of Mexico over the years, but nothing compared to this. There was a rich and distinctive blend of traditions and history here, including the Maya civilization and Spanish conquistadors. Much less English was spoken, and once again, we regretted that we could not speak Spanish.

I was worried about my stomach, as it was starting to cramp badly. I wasn't sure if it was nerves, my IBS flaring, or the start of what some of the others had picked up. I made a big mistake in leaving the B&B, as I soon began cramping severely and running for the bathroom soon after. As it turned out, I had food poisoning and dysentery. (I blamed that Sonoran hot dog! Never again.) I was green by then but tried to keep quiet and tag along. We stopped at a restaurant, where the others had margaritas and Mexican food. They were feeling pretty good and were celebrating our good fortune. I sipped Sprite and nibbled on saltines, and I visited the restroom a few more times. All I wanted was my bed, but I was trying not to say too much, as I didn't want everyone to feel they should go back because of me. Later, after we finally made it back, a few others came down sick as well. I went straight to bed.

My Resolve Began to Crumble

Richard found some Cream of Wheat and made it for me. I was so thankful for that, as it had always been my comfort food. Over the years, as my IBS flared, Cream of Wheat and Saltines generally were all I could keep down. I spent most of the days remaining confined to bed. I cried quietly but tried to hide it. It was all becoming too much for me. Richard held me and reassured me that everything would be all right.

Mary Jane called, and when I heard her voice, I started sobbing. I was violently sick; I could not eat and was getting weaker by the moment, and I was not sleeping either. My resolve was disintegrating, and that upset me even more. I wished I could reach out and have her hold me. I am sure it was just as difficult for her to hear me breaking down and not be able to do anything about it.

I was up sick several times that night. I cried out, praying in desperation, "Lord, I cannot do this anymore. Please make it stop. I cannot travel on airplanes and taxis tomorrow like this." All night long, I prayed while running back and forth to the bathroom. When morning came, I was completely drained. I didn't have an ounce of strength left in me. We went to breakfast, and everyone asked how I was doing. I started crying at the table. I could not even drink fluids at that point. I felt humiliated that I wasn't able to hold it together in front of them, I felt like I was losing it. They all comforted and supported me.

My aunt and uncle, Janet and Chuck, and Tina and Joella all flew out before Richard and I—we had the last flight out, and I lay down until we had to leave for the airport. Richard led me in a fog; I felt disembodied at that point. I have read passages in books that were similar to this, but it was another thing entirely to experience it for myself.

We arrived at the airport and checked our bags, only to find our flight was delayed for three and a half hours. We waited in a daze. Richard and I were to fly from Merida to Guadalajara to Phoenix. For some reason, there was a mix-up when we checked in, and they changed our flight to go through Mexico City instead. We were worried about missing the next flight and asked if they could hold the connecting flight to Phoenix. At first, they would not, but after about eleven people spoke up, they decided to hold the plane. We had to sprint from one plane to the other, which was already loaded and ready to go.

When we landed in Mexico City, we learned the flight to Phoenix had already taken off! It was now nine o'clock Friday night, and we were stuck in Mexico City. Once again, I lost it. How much more was I supposed to take? Enough already! I needed to be home; I needed my daughters. Richard tried everything he could do to get us on any other flight to the States, even LA, but there were none. We were sent back to the baggage terminal; our luggage was not there, as it had been tagged through to the Phoenix flight that had left. Airline staff said we could wait in line to be put up in a hotel near the airport. We called our family, who couldn't believe we were stuck yet again.

I laid down and prayed. Praise God, my prayers about the diarrhea were answered. From the moment I had to travel, it had completely stopped. Thank God, I didn't have to deal with that. For the first time in a week and a half, I slept like the dead, a much-needed gift as well. I awoke to find myself feeling halfway human again. Sleep made such a difference in my mental state, and I had a little more strength. We returned to the airport and I was able to eat an Egg McMuffin. It was delicious and went a long way to helping my physical and emotional states.

On the flight to Phoenix, I went through a lot of guilt about the times in the past two days when I had cracked. I usually was strong; I had been the pillar of strength for my family in crisis situations. Here, I ended up a weak basket case, and I felt horrible about this. My rational side said, "Come on. Lucy. You went through the eye of the storm and back. You did not eat for close to a week, had no sleep for a week and a half, and experienced dysentery. For God's sake, cut yourself some slack." I knew this was true, yet it has taken time for me to get over the guilt of breaking down like that. I don't know why that is, but I felt like it meant my faith might not be strong enough. Maybe it was because I didn't see anyone else break down. In sharing this with Richard, he said that the morning we arrived at In Ka'an, he was the first one up, and he talked to Bonnie. He admitted that he was in tears then; it all had caught up with him once we were safe. This made me feel much better. Tina also confided in me later that she broke down in private that morning also. Hearing that we all broke down in our own ways helped me to accept that I had too.

Home at Last

I was never so relieved as when we finally landed in Phoenix. Our family and friends were standing there with a large banner, welcoming us home. Even now, it brings tears to my eyes when I remember what this homecoming was like. I had never been so happy to see them in all my life—to hold my daughters again and my mother, my father. We were touched and shocked to see that Chuck, Jan, Tina, and Joella were there as well, all with T-shirts that read: "Wilma—Bite Me"! They had arrived in Phoenix at one in the morning but still came to the airport to welcome us. "We started this together, we will end it together!" Amen!

As I think back on this ordeal, I recognize that I learned much through this experience. We have no real control over the circumstances in our lives. We pull together and seek guidance from above to help us make the right decisions. We must think smart and put our faith and trust in God, and He *will* pull us through; He will lead us down the dark path into the light. I also learned how important it is doing life in community with others, we were never meant to go it alone. We need each other.

Nothing is impossible for God; I must always remember this. No circumstance is too great for Him to handle. I find peace in knowing that

He is with me. Janet wrote something on the banner that will stay with me forever: "Swept up and carried in the hands of God." Not one of us doubted that we were being cared for throughout our journey together. I was shown that no matter the situation or circumstance, I will come through it. While I had seen this before in other areas of my life, this reinforced it in a mighty way.

Reference

1. Huie, Jonathan Lockwood. "Strength Quotes and Sayings Quotes about Strength by Jonathan Lockwood Huie." Joyful Living through Conscious Choice. http://www.jonathanlockwoodhuie.com/quotes/strength. Accessed June 2019
2. Lewis, C.S. The Problem of Pain (New York: Macmillan, 1962), 152

7

My Artistic Journey

I paint not by sight but by faith. Faith gives you sight.
—Amos Ferguson

What lies behind us and what lies before us are tiny
matters, compared to what lies within us.
—Ralph Waldo Emerson

Throughout my life, my artistic expression has been a very important part of who I am, who I was created to be. It has helped me to process as I have traveled through many of my most difficult trials and greatest joys. I have been a creative all of my life; my mother and daughters are as well and even my father. I mentioned that my parents instilled in me a passion for the outdoors and to seek the beauty all around me, from the tiniest flower and snowflake to the grandest mountains. At the family cabin when I was a child, my dad photographed snowflakes on the deck railing with a telephoto lens. He used black-and-white film and did his own developing. I was enthralled with watching those images appear on the white page, little by little, as if by magic in the makeshift darkroom. These photos of the snowflakes filled me with wonder and awe—the detail and intricacy in their patterns, all of them distinctly unique. What a moment!

Art has always been therapeutic for me and still is. It's not only an outlet; it also feeds my soul. We creatives are made to create; we must create, or we grow stifled. It's a drive set in us from deep within. I later learned that God chose us to create, to further creation, to invite us into cocreating. I am not implying that we are equal in any sense, only that I'm deeply thankful for this gift, and I show my gratitude by using the gift. *Now hear me strongly*: we are *all* created with special gifts and talents—all of us—and we must be careful to not covet another's. Each is equally important, each is to be used for God's glory and for making an impact in the lives others.

> Each of you should use whatever gift you have received to serve others, as faithful stewards of God's grace in its various forms.

—Peter 4:10 (NIV)

Please don't limit yourself in the way you think about your talent; don't wonder whether it is good enough. Are you a natural encourager, a prayer warrior? Is hospitality your gift or leadership? Is it writing, photography, healing, serving, giving, cooking, sewing, teaching, or preaching? Are you a visionary? Do you have a trade skill? Is your gift with children or the elderly or counseling others? These talents are rich and diverse. And the list goes on. Yes, you have a gift and talent by divine design and are called to use it.

When I was young, my creative outlets were pencil and charcoal. Of course, art was my favorite subject in high school, and I was fortunate to have a wonderfully inspiring art teacher. While I had a passion for it, for some reason, seeing it as a career path never crossed my mind. Maybe seeing my parents—a talented photographer and a watercolor artist—not use these talents as primary professions had an impact on my mindset. My marrying at nineteen, having babies, and birthing a business with my husband shortly thereafter impacted my time to pursue creative outlets as well. There was no time or desire for college, even though I had straight A's in high school and was encouraged to go. Richard tried college classes briefly, when we were in our first townhouse, but it was impossible for him to work back-to-back shifts, support our household, and go to college too. He was burning the candle at both ends and had to give it up. During my time at our company, my creative outlets were on hold; there was no time. I became stifled inside; I felt stuck somehow and, at times, anxious or unsettled. A deeply rooted need to create filled my heart, and there was great frustration in having no time to express it. I had no idea just how much art nourished me until I picked it up again.

We moved into our new home after Richard's cancer scare. I was having fun with the decorating and always felt that if things had been different, it would have been great to become an interior designer. I decided I wanted to paint a mural on the walls in our home, but it was important to see if I could paint first.

In 2003, I expressed this to my mom and my friend Mary Jane. They encouraged me, and we decided to meet on Monday mornings and paint in my dining room. Mom and Mary Jane are watercolor and oil painters, and I looked forward to learning from them. I planned on trying to work a four-day workweek and create some balance, giving me this creative time. Since I wanted to paint a mural, I thought, *I should try to paint on the same surface, then.* I asked Richard to bring a big piece of demolition drywall home from work. It was about four feet tall, with jagged edges. I bought a pile of acrylic craft paints—it's wild to look back on that now. I jumped right in, and with their coaching, tackled a tropical scene.

I found I had a real talent for it and completely enjoyed creating in that way. I loved painting more than words can describe. Richard was surprised to see what I had created and became the most supportive husband toward my art. He immediately gifted me with an easel and a professional acrylic paint set. From the first time I put brush to canvas, I knew this was what I was supposed to be doing. This was who I was. I had no idea where it would take me—even now, the path continues to unfold—but I knew this: I must paint! The more I painted, the more a deep passion welled up inside me and filled me with a sense of purpose. My heart was bursting with profound joy and deep emotion. I have felt this way ever since while creating. It became very clear to me that this was part of my calling, my outreach, and that God wanted to use this. I had no idea how I would do this or what it would look like, but I knew it to be real at the core of my being. I sought to learn everything I could and was like a sponge, soaking up knowledge anywhere I could find it. I took workshops, read books, visited museums and galleries, and watched videos. Then, I would try it. I began to pray before, after, and during each painting. From an early age, I have been drawn to the incredible work of the great masters, especially the Hudson River Valley painters, such as Thomas Cole and Fredrick Church. Studying these artists and their handling of paints, their mastery of atmosphere and light, along with capturing a sense of the divine, continues to influence my work today.

Out back, we had a detached RV garage with a bonus room. It was intended to be a game room but was really a big, unorganized junk pile. We had planned to take a two-week travel-trailer road trip adventure for our family vacation. Without my knowing, Richard was working with Mom and a carpenter to pull off an ambitious while-you-were-out studio conversion for my birthday. We returned from our road trip to a gift from Richard that would forever change my life—my own art studio. I could hardly believe my eyes! There was a place for my easel and storage, slots for canvases, a sink for cleanup and two great rolling cabinet sections I could pull out and sit at with a barstool. This was the best gift I had ever received.

Richard has always demonstrated support of me and my art in such fantastic ways, always believing in me. Mom, Mary Jane, and I moved into the studio and began painting together; I was at my easel, and they were at the two rolling workstations. How wonderful to be able to leave everything out that I was working on—no more packing everything up at dinnertime. We have so many cherished memories from this wonderful time of creating together.

Shortly after we came through the hurricane misadventure, I stepped back into this wonderful studio and created a painting called *Through the Eye of the Storm* to send to Bonnie and Pat of In Ka'an, as a thank-you gift for taking such great care of us. This was also a purging and healing for me. I find painting helps to heal my soul. Somehow, as I process and convey emotion through my paintings and stories, a release takes place. God works on my heart and ministers strongly to me as my brush and pen move.

About a year after I started painting, the stress of our demolition business continued full throttle. This pulled me from my painting, but the company was more important at that point. We began questioning why I was still working full time in our business. I didn't need to work any longer financially, and we wondered if maybe it was time for me to step out of the business. While I yearned to do this, it also frightened me. Who would watch our money like I did? Richard and I prayed about it and discussed our options extensively. We finally decided this was the right decision. I would be home for our children, who were in high school, as these were such defining years in the life of a child. I would be able to create a better haven for my husband to come home to as well. We wanted to create a healthy separation of work and home for our relationship, and this would better help him to leave work at the door. This would also allow me to devote more time to my painting, which was extremely appealing to me. We conducted several interviews, searched diligently for a replacement, and finally found the perfect person. She was a CFO with an accounting degree who we had to pay three times as much as me. We joke all the time that when Richard retires, he has to come to work for me for pennies also. He assures me he will.

About the time I was stepping out of our demolition company, around 2005, my uncle, Colin, who had funded us, said, "Give it a year, and your art is going to be your business."

"No way," I said. "I am done with that. I want no part of turning my art into a business."

He was, however, right on the money once again. Shortly after that conversation, I took one of my acrylic paintings in for framing. This framer happened to be opening a gallery on Main Street in Scottsdale, on Gallery Row. He wanted to see more of my work, and before I knew it, my artwork was hanging on prestigious Main Street. This went on for a few years as my talent and skills grew, and then, the severe market downturn came in 2008, and the gallery closed. Many people were not buying art when they were worrying about being able to pay their mortgages or seeing their investment portfolios cut in half. This was a difficult time for me. I kept hearing in my spirit as I prayed, *Just keep painting, and trust me.* It seemed like this went on forever.

I had been painting in acrylic for about four years when I went to an arts league meeting I was involved with and heard a fine-art consultant speak on the business of art. I was eager for more and sought her out. She came to evaluate my work, along with witnessing my passion and drive and raw talent. She decided to become my coach and consultant. She asked a lot of questions, such as where I wanted to go with my art, what it meant to me, and why I painted. Many of my answers were the same as they are now: I want to bring hope and beauty, light and inspiration, encouragement, and a sense of grace. I want to capture memories and invite viewers into the beauty. I want to impact the world through my art.

I want to get my work out there in a big and powerful way and gently share my faith through my painting and through my writing as well to inspire.

Based on this, it was her opinion that I needed to switch to oil painting. She said there was a ceiling in acrylic, whether we agreed with it or not. I wasn't happy to hear this, but after diligent thought and prayer, I laid down my acrylic paints and picked up oil painting overnight. The learning curve was *so* much greater than I expected. I experienced much frustration at not knowing how to accomplish what I wanted. Oil paint dries a lot slower, and the colors can get muddied easily. Some are transparent, whereas acrylics are opaque; you can put any layer over another. In oil, you are able to see through many of the color layers, and there is such a richness to them. I loved the vibrancy of oil painting, though, and when I finally learned to manipulate and apply them properly, I was hooked.

My consultant knew I was preparing to travel to Italy with my family for the first time, and she knew I loved sharing little stories about each painting. She is the one who first challenged me to bring a travel journal to capture everything: what I thought, what I felt, the significance of the area and details, what drew me to paint a scene and why. The storyteller of fine art in me was born and has been evolving ever since. The stories posted with my paintings are my unique way of bringing you along on the journey with me, both on canvas and in word. I'd love to share a recent painting and its story. I think this captures the interplay between my creative outlets of painting, storytelling, and journaling, with my faith thread interwoven throughout.

The Invitation, 48 x 32 oil, Lucy Dickens

It's not often a painting title and story come to me clearly before the painting itself. It's such a beautiful thing when it does. I knew I wanted to paint a large Aspen painting, but just could not "see" it. Feeling frustrated and creatively stifled, I got into prayer, reading, and started journaling once again over a period of days. Why do I stop writing when I am so often spoken to when my pen moves?

Through this process, *The Invitation* came clearly into view and then these words: *Seeing the pure beauty before us, aren't we invited in? Do our hearts not long, even ache, to step within, to be enveloped, to experience, to become one with the beauty? Is it not a picture of a greater call placed deep within our hearts, a longing, for the beauty of creation, of the Creator himself?*

Then, stepping before my canvas and my photos, I could clearly "see" the vision given to me, the one meant for *The*

Invitation. How do I express my deep gratitude for this?
In the only way I know how: by sharing her with you.

This storytelling has become a huge part of who I am as an artist today. I most enjoy painting in a series from my travel journeys, bringing viewers along on the journey with me through painted images and my written story that accompanies each painting. I hope to evoke feelings of serenity and grace, a scene to transport you to another place and time, exploring the mystery within, to capture memories and those fleeting moments of beauty. There is a story evolving all around us, and my hope is to inspire and encourage you through my images and words.

> "Her realism is not about reproducing a scene, but rather capturing those special moments with all the accompanying magic. In this regard, she has a gift. She is able to reveal spirit and enable viewers to be part of the experience as she makes a special connection with her subject matter and honors its essence." People respond. (Kublin 2015)

I paint predominantly because I'm drawn to moments that take my breath away. Those moments of beauty that cause me to feel, to reflect, and to give thanks draw me in. It's those fleeting visions that I strive to capture. The interplay of light and shadow draws me deeply into a scene. What does the light touch? What is hiding in the shadows? How do they dance? I love the sound of the wind in the trees or water gently lapping the shore, a babbling brook, and the dance of dragonflies darting to and fro. It's all entrances me. I think of how I can convey these experiences in oil paint and in word.

Around 2011, I decided to participate in the huge Sonoran Arts League's Hidden in the Hills Artist Studio Tour. I had been praying about whether this was something I should do. In fact, I had been in a constant state of prayer over this and was feeling unsettled and distressed because not much was happening with my art in shows or sales. I kept asking God, "What am I missing? Am I supposed to be doing something different? Am I not hearing You right?" Over and over again, I heard in my spirit, *Just keep painting, and trust me.* Later, I heard, *Be ready.* Well, that was an answer, wasn't it? It just wasn't the one I wanted to hear. Richard reminded me it *was* my answer, and it *was* enough. Rest in it; trust in it. Why was this so hard for me?

Why couldn't I be content just to paint? I *was* making an impact through my stories and newsletters, he said. Sometimes the answer to our prayers is, *No, not yet.* We can be so impatient, can't we? I know I can be. I was reading *Streams in the Desert* by Mrs. Charles E. Cowman in the middle of the night, and God showed me this: *Lucy, I will show you if you veer off course. I will guide you back if you make a wrong turn. You are on the right path. Just trust me. I know the plans I have for you; my plans are not your plans. Rest in me. I've got you.* I received this deep in my soul, and a peace washed over me. I was able to rest in God and to sleep.

The next morning, I awoke in a calm state, even in the midst of a lot going on, even during the wait for my breast biopsy results, even when my computer crashed completely, I rested in Him.

> I will instruct you and teach you the way you should go; I
> will counsel you with My loving eye upon you.
>
> —Psalm 32:8 (NIV)

I put out an email blast to the arts league artists, sharing my paintings and my website, along with the stories that accompany each of them. I let them know I wanted to participate in the show and was looking for a studio to join. All the while, I was praying, *Your will, not mine, Lord. Open the doors I should walk through; close those I should not.* I have found this to be a very effective prayer.

I received a few invitations for interviews. Then, I received an email from the host studio artist Elizabeth Cox. If you are not part of a host studio, you cannot participate unless one invites you in.

She said, "I do not have an opening right now, but I have a Christian Artists group if you would like to come."

I burst into tears right then and there. I had no idea such a thing existed. It seemed a direct answer to prayer. She invited me to visit her and then have lunch after my interviews. We instantly clicked. I shared my art and faith journey, and she shared hers. What a beautiful experience. I shared that I had just found a studio. It was limited, but it was an indoor space, which was hard to come by.

Later, she contacted me: "If I were to offer you a space here in my guest casita, would you take it?"

I couldn't believe it! Not only did she have a very successful studio with a large following, but she offered me the whole casita to showcase my work in. This was a dream come true, another answer to prayer, and then to learn her studio was filled with Christian artists—what an incredible unfolding of events. God placed me right where He wanted me; thank you, Jesus! The show that year was hugely successful for us all. How wonderful to be able to pray together over the event and over all who set foot on the property that they would feel welcome and cherished.

This became our heart space and philosophy, and our success grew year by year. My collectors continued to grow and expand, and I spent much time driving across town for these art events, league meetings, meeting with clients, art installations, and more.

Richard always wanted to live out in Carefree or North Scottsdale, with the sheer beauty of the picturesque giant boulders and high desert. His love for outdoor adventuring influenced this as well. During one of my shows, he drove around, looking at property. He brought me to see one that I thought was horrible. This home was stripped, abandoned, and unlivable and even had a bobcat living in the courtyard. The inside had low ceilings, choppy rooms, and no real views. Every floor height was different, and it was in complete disrepair. The inside was dark and dreary; many of the walls were painted flat black with curlicue stenciling on the ceilings and floors, and it had black chandeliers.

Even as an artist, I somehow could not see past the darkness or the enormous renovation project this would entail. I told Richard he was out of his mind and that we weren't in the market anyway—but apparently, he was. Approximately eight months later, as I was preparing for the show again, he pleaded, "Please let's look at it again. It has gone bank-owned and has dropped again in price. Look at the lot, with its incredible views and the location. Ignore the house. I'm in demolition. We can do anything with it."

Well, I did return again, trying to keep an open mind. The bones of this block home were good, especially the courtyard, but the walls were so high, like a fortress, that I couldn't see the beautiful views. Stepping into the courtyard, the front door was straight ahead. To the right was a door to the master bedroom, which I found odd.

Ever the salesman, this is how Richard convinced me: "Now imagine this—you walk into this beautiful courtyard with the walls lowered and enter your own gallery space. The back opens into your working studio. We will even cut in a large picture window looking out at Boulder Pile," which was a large, picturesque boulder outcropping.

Ah, I could see it. *What a dream that would be,* I thought wistfully. He knew just what to say to woo me, always did.

We purchased the property but waited for two years until we felt it was the right time to start on a design-and-renovation plan. Richard and I would drive out, climb an extension ladder to the roof, and daydream of when we would build and what we would do. We would watch as the sun set, casting a warm glow on the surrounding granite mountains. The glorious moon rose behind us as we gazed in wonder, glasses of wine in our hands. The twinkling city lights emerged in the distance.

We found a great local design builder who helped our dream become a reality. It took about two years, including demolition and design. I knew from the beginning that I would want to be a host studio for the annual art event, and we designed this house and my gallery studio with that in mind. We created an incredible Mediterranean retreat, capturing special elements from all our travels, including a stunning brick barrel ceiling over the kitchen.

My gallery and studio space are a dream; sometimes, I still have to pinch myself to remind me that this is all real. I feel a little like Cinderella at the ball.

My artist team knew I was planning to leave them, and as the show closed that year, I said my tearful goodbyes. I fully expected I would have to find all new artists to join me at my new studio. Then something changed for Beth and her husband—a grandbaby was born in North Carolina. They immediately bought a little bungalow near their daughter and started renovating it. After spending more and more time there, they made a tough decision to downsize here. This meant not hosting anymore; she asked to join me, and I had room to bring over most of the other artists.

I was so thankful and excited that we would still be showing together. We were all family.

A local magazine ran a renovation story on our home, inviting their readers to see our house in person during the art event. They had run a wonderful feature article on me and my art the year before. Also in 2016, my painting *Joyful* made the cover of the event program directory. Our first show here was a huge success, and because of this, I was asked to be on the Cave Creek home tour, with many other visitors through my home, gallery, and studio. The following years were an even greater success.

We decided long ago that our home would be a place to welcome friends and strangers alike, a place where, we prayed, all would feel welcome and cherished and would feel God's love and presence. Our home and all of us are covered in prayer for protection as well. *Bring all those who should be here, Lord,* I prayed. *May they be impacted. And keep from coming all those who should not be here.* We opened our home to much more than art events as well.

Being in this location has been an unbelievable experience; to live in this artist community, surrounded with art lovers is wonderful. Being always at the ready at a moment's notice for visits by appointment has made a huge impact on my art business. I receive calls for appointments to visit my gallery studio all the time, and I have a part-time assistant. This allows me to be at my easel, creating, more of the time, which is just where I want to be. Exposure has continued to increase, including larger shows, an ever-expanding collector base, along with gallery representation.

Creating art feeds my soul. When I am in the flow, I am in God, with the Holy Spirit leading me as my muse. I feel such joy. Creating feels so necessary; it's a deep-rooted need for me and for me to share with others. I feel a frustration or a longing when I am not creating, and I know I am also called to create and release.

I once dug through a trash heap in Mexico when we were on a mission trip, building for those in need. Why? I felt there must be some shred of beauty there. *What can I use from the discarded to beautify the simple concrete stoop,* I thought, *something to help take it from house to home, welcoming them in?* I stumbled upon broken shards of colorful pottery. Maybe if I found enough, I could make a mosaic stoop, pressing the pieces into the concrete as it dried. What about these broken curved pavers? Could I stand them up and make a lined pathway to the stoop? I could spread gravel in between that was sifted from the dirt to make the stucco. It was then, on top of the trash heap, that I heard, *You are called to be a bringer of light and beauty.* Aha! This spoke deeply to my soul. I wrote it out and have it posted next to my easel. I will never forget it. *Lord, may I always bring light and beauty to the world around me.*

References

1. Amos Ferguson. AZQuotes.com, Wind and Fly LTD, 2021. https://www.azquotes.com/quote/585594, accessed August 31, 2021.
2. Henry David Thoreau. AZQuotes.com, Wind and Fly LTD, 2021. https://www.azquotes.com/quote/294032, accessed August 31, 2021.
3. Cowman, Mrs. Charles E., and James Reimann. 2016. *Streams in the Desert: 366 Daily Devotional Readings*. Grand Rapids: Zondervan.
4. Kublin, Donna. 2015. "The Circle of Gifts." *Images AZ* magazine, September 2015.
5. Cowman, Mrs. Charles E., and James Reimann. 2016. *Streams in the Desert: 366 Daily Devotional Readings*. Grand Rapids: Zondervan.
6. Cowman, Mrs. Charles E., and James Reimann. 2016. *Streams in the Desert: 366 Daily Devotional Readings*. Grand Rapids: Zondervan.

8

A CRUSHING BLOW

I have told you all this so that you may have peace in me.
Here on earth you will have many trials and sorrows.
But take heart because I have overcome the world.
—John 16:33 (NIV)

It's interesting to write about so many different stories unfolding simultaneously throughout my life, from the joy of painting to the trauma of relational strife to natural disasters. I back up now to 2008 and a tragic and defining moment in the life of my marriage and our family. This happened a few years after Hurricane Wilma and fairly early into my artistic journey.

Richard and I had begun to grow complacent in our faith once again, living one foot in and one foot out. We let the stresses of life and distractions take over. We attended church and a neighborhood group Bible study, when we were available, and we enjoyed that, along with the friendships found there. However, we quickly forgot the messages, and we certainly weren't trying to implement them or let the teachings impact our lives. We spent a lot of money, indulged ourselves frequently, and went everywhere we wanted, including a lot of time spent camping and off-roading in the sand dunes. We grew a bit wild. There were fun times, but there certainly were plenty of red flags and danger signs in many areas of our lives as well, although we seemed oblivious to them. Richard and I were not close and not communicating deeply. Our differences became points of contention. Too easily, we became angry and bickered with each other. I remember then him saying we just tolerated each other. This was crushing to me, quite a blow to my heart.

That Valentine's Day, I received a call from Richard; he had been in a motorcycle accident. He tried downplaying it—until I arrived at the hospital. While riding his bike in downtown Phoenix—something he promised he never would do—a truck suddenly pulled out in front of him. Before he could react, he was flying through the air, landing in the bed of this truck. Landing there probably saved his life, as there was heavy traffic all around. His nose was dislocated; he needed plastic surgery and over a hundred stitches in his face, and he had a broken thumb. Richard was very fortunate. After being thankful that he was alive, I was angry, furious in fact. I didn't like who he was becoming and who he was spending time with on the bike and how dangerous it was. We fought about this and the bike; tears flowed profusely. In hindsight, God was trying to get his attention once again—another time his life was spared.

Soon afterward, a phone call came that changed everything. A husband called to tell me that something was going on between his wife and my husband.

"You have to talk to him about it," he said

"*What?* No, I can't believe it. I won't believe it!" I cried. Richard wasn't home, but I quickly called him, my heart clenching tight, asking, "Is it true?"

"I am on my way home," he said.

Deep down in my heart, I knew; my heart was scorched, as if by fire. Through my tears, shock, and disbelief, he began to come clean. This couple had been having marital problems for some time. This woman and my husband began talking about the problems she had with her husband. It started out with Richard trying to help them. The more they talked, the more a connection began between her and Richard, with him sharing his frustrations with me as well. They began to meet in person, alone, to talk, and things escalated further—an embrace, a kiss. Then, by the grace of God, her husband intercepted a text before it went too far beyond that.

Richard then poured out everything—all the things he had been hiding from me, from everyone, about him battling secret depression and feeling like he couldn't tell anyone about it. The tears poured as he shared the unbelievable pressure he had felt to take care of everyone—our family, extended family, the company, the livelihood of our employees, and so on. He felt the weight of it all crushing down on him to the point that he could hardly stand up under it all. He shared some traumatic childhood experiences and abuses that I had never known. These experiences left scars with him, not unlike my own. He had his own lies lodged deep and arrows to be battled.

"Do you realize what you have done?" I cried. "What kind of a man are you? Do you have no honor?"

The husband of the woman involved promised to tell everyone, everywhere—and he did, even embellished.

"You have to tell your daughters before they hear from someone else," I said. "How could you do this to me, to us?" I was devastated and humiliated, destroyed beyond belief. In that moment, I cried out to Jesus, "Lord, help me. This is way beyond anything I can deal with. This is all yours. I cannot save my marriage. I cannot make my husband love me. Jesus, move in this situation. I beg you. I have absolutely no control. There is nothing I can do. I give all control to you, Jesus; move in my marriage. Tell me what to do. Please reach my husband!"

Did I still love him? Of course. Did I still see the man deep inside that Richard hadn't found yet? Absolutely. Jesus showed me a glimpse of him often. Yet my insides felt absolutely shredded.

"You *have* to go to your father and your brother, and tell them what you have done," I insisted. "Confess and seek their help." Praise God he did, many men would not have, they would have walked right out the door.

Richard painfully climbed into his truck and headed straight over to see his father and poured out everything to him. From there, he drove over to his older brother, Ron's, house to speak to him. Richard poured his heart out once again. He later told me that they cried in each other's arms for what felt like an eternity.

His brother talked to him for a very long time about all he had done, the deceptions, and his faith or lack thereof. His brother questioned Richard's relationship with Jesus. Richard then met with our church neighborhood group leader, whom he deeply respected. He confided in this man and sought godly counsel and support. This man also questioned Richard's relationship with Christ—what it was like, how he felt about it, and if Richard truly accepted Jesus Christ into his heart as his Lord and Savior.

Richard said he didn't think so; he thought that he was mostly going through the motions because he *did* want his marriage to work. He was always doing just enough to get by, attempting to keep the peace.

Sometimes, he came very close in faith with these big wake-up calls, but he always fell away again all too easily.

"Do you want to invite Jesus in now?" his mentor asked.

"Yes," Richard said through his tears.

Together, they prayed the sinner's prayer. Richard later shared it with me; it was something similar to this:

> Father, I believe that Jesus Christ is Your Son; that He died on the cross and rose again to pay the penalty for my sins and to reconcile me to You. I have sinned against you and confess, Lord. Please forgive me. I want you, Jesus, to come into my life and into my heart as my Lord and Savior.

Richard described an unexplainable peace that washed over him in that moment, a filling.

I would describe the same thing when it happened for me. Other accounts may vary, but we all *know* because something infinitely significant happens inside.

What happens at conversion—that moment when you finally believe and let it all go, when you invite Christ into your heart and your life as Lord and Savior? Finally, you believe that He died as penalty for *your* sins and rose again on the third day, reconciling *you* to the Father. You cry out in sincere repentance, asking for forgiveness—and forgiveness is granted. It is an indescribable experience, this amazing thing that happens, to those who do not believe or who haven't experienced it for themselves.

I'm not trying to convince you of anything. That's not my job or anyone else's, for that matter; it is God's job. Jesus enables a heart to believe. He removes the blinders from the eyes and ears. I am only to be obedient in sharing my story and my experiences and let God do with it what He may. It is at this moment of acceptance and conversion that you are filled with the Holy Spirit.

> And I will ask the Father, and He will give you another advocate to help you and be with you forever the Spirit of truth. The world cannot accept Him because it neither

sees Him nor knows Him. But you know Him, for He
lives with you and will be in you.

—John 14:16–17 NLT)

You are transformed from the inside out.

In Him you also, when you heard the word of truth, the
gospel of your salvation, and believed in him, were sealed
with the promised Holy Spirit.

—Ephesians 1:13 (ESV)

The Holy Spirit lives in us and sanctifies and cleanses us. We have
been pardoned. He guides and coaches, leads and transforms, convicts and
teaches us to live wisely. He even speaks to us through others. He develops
in us the fruits of the spirit—love, joy, peace, patience, kindness, goodness,
faithfulness, gentleness, and self-control.

Through the Spirit we accept God's love and are filled
with it. Even more, He validates us directly to God with
groaning too deep for words. He intercedes for us when
we don't know how to pray. (Moore)

All our messes are not fixed in those moments. There are consequences
to our actions, and depending on the circumstances, deep hurts exist, and
trust needs to be rebuilt. The Holy Spirit comes in at that moment, and
you are forgiven, but the transformation is a process over time, much time.
We were far from where the Holy Spirit wanted to bring us. But this was
the beginning of that journey.

Richard came home absolutely crushed and knelt before me with his
head in my lap. He was sobbing at all the pain he had ever caused me and
wanted desperately to make it right.

Later that night, as I was getting ready for bed, he asked me, "Do you
want me to leave?"

"*No*," I said adamantly, "you need to stay *right here* and face this.

You need to make it right. I'm not going to push you out the door and potentially into another's arms. That is not the way."

I easily could have told him to get out and never come back. Part of me screamed it! Yet even in that moment, I *listened* to God and knew it was wrong; it would be the beginning of the end, all of it unraveling. I knew it. I promised God I would do it *His* way; mine had failed miserably before.

The next day, Richard had to tell our girls. First was Amanda; she was still at home and in early high school. It was absolutely heart-wrenching for all of us. Richard could barely get through it. We all were sobbing as he confessed to our beautiful daughter. She took him in her arms, crying and holding him, and then she ran to her room and brought back and played the song "Mighty to Save" for him. I get chills, even today, every time I hear that song. This was one of the biggest pictures of grace I had ever experienced. She was here; she was able to look him in the eye and see the true and pure remorse, the anguish. For him, it was not about being upset with being caught; it was a complete and total brokenness and despair. She saw the rawness of it all.

Alicia, away at college in LA, did not have the same reaction or the benefit of looking into his eyes. She received a phone call from her dad, in which he confessed. In one moment, he came crashing down off her pedestal and shattered on the ground. "Put Mom on the phone!" she demanded.

I don't remember what I said; it was all a blur. I had cried a river of tears and was fairly numb by then. She seemed angry that *I* was not angry; she couldn't understand. She was not there to see that I *was* angry—furious, in fact—and hurt, then sick, then sobbing, then just numb again. I went through the gamut of emotions, grieving what was, what is.

It was *many* weeks before Alicia would speak to her father again.

Amanda, seeing what was happening between her sister and her dad, asked us to send her to LA so she could be with and talk to Alicia. We immediately sent her out to California. I'm not sure how those conversations went, but I knew they needed to be together; both were grieving and processing.

Richard's brother offered to meet with him weekly to mentor him; they began immediately. He was challenged to get into daily Bible reading, starting with the proverb of the day. There are thirty-one chapters in the book of Proverbs, and he suggested reading one a day and repeating this every month. It's amazing that you can continue reading Proverbs each month, and a different verse will grab your heart, based on what you are going through at the time. This only took five to ten minutes and was a good way to get in the habit of daily reading.

Well, Richard thought his brother had said to read Psalms, and when he got to Psalm 32, he broke completely over those words. God knew exactly what he needed to read on this day. Richard considers these words one of his most important life verses.

> Blessed is the one whose transgressions are forgiven, whose sins are covered. Blessed is the one whose sin the Lord does not count against them and in whose spirit is no deceit. When I kept silent, my bones wasted away through my groaning all day long. For day and night your hand was heavy on me; my strength was sapped as in the heat of summer. Then I acknowledged my sin to You and did not cover up my iniquity. I said, "I will confess my transgressions to the Lord." And You forgave the guilt of my sin. Therefore, let all the faithful pray to You while You may be found; surely the rising of the mighty waters will not reach them. You are my hiding place; You will protect me from trouble and surround me with songs of deliverance. I will instruct You and teach You in the way you should go; I will counsel You with my loving eye on you. Do not be like the horse or the mule, which have no understanding but must be controlled by bit and bridle or they will not come to you. Many are the woes of the wicked, but the Lord's unfailing love surrounds the one who trusts in him. Rejoice in the LORD and be glad, You are righteous; sing, all you who are upright in heart!
>
> —Psalm 32 (NIV)

As I watched him reading the Bible every day, I finally decided to start as well. We began reading the same thing each day so we could talk about it together. It was time we really understood what we said we believed.

The Necessary Changes

We both went for Christian counseling, and he continued by himself for a very long time. Yes, he was repentant (which means to turn and go in the other direction) and meant it, but this was no easy road. It was gruesome, raw, and very painful, and he felt attacked on all sides. He had to face this daily at work, in friendship circles, and at home, with all the memories, accusations from others, and temptations. Richard immediately quit drinking, knowing that had contributed to our problems as well. It was this crisis and these few pivotal men who came alongside him that brought about the turning point in his life—that, and the way I stayed by him, despite it all.

This was incredibly hard for me as well, facing everyone and standing by him. I know many saw me as weak or foolish back then. *Let me tell you* that it took a mountain of strength—strength that I could only find in God—to give me the courage to stand firm through all of this and do it God's way.

We had to evaluate the situations we put ourselves into, who were we spending our time with, and whether it was healthy for us or not. He sold his sand rail (an off-road dune buggy), and we stopped going to the dunes and to certain parties and events. Richard chose all of this on his own; I didn't tell him what to do. I just prayed unendingly and trusted God to work on his heart. This was not a judgment on any of those friends, although some of them took it that way; it was only a recognition that these places were not healthy for *us* at that point. We needed to guard and protect our fragile healing while working on our marriage. Repairing the damage was most important to us.

We implemented safe boundaries or guardrails for both of us. We were never alone with someone of the opposite sex; we always communicated where we were; and we had each other's passwords to everything and permission to check anything at any time.

Painting was very therapeutic for me, not only during the time of healing my marriage but also throughout my faith journey. For countless hours, I would lose myself in front of the easel, with my faith music serenading me in the background, ministering to my heart as I painted—and waited as my heart began to heal. Creating fed my soul; it was such a powerful therapy. For hours upon hours, I would lose myself in my paintings and my thoughts. This became quite a prayerful time for me, an infusing of these emotions and reflections in my work. My painting journey walked hand in hand with my faith journey throughout this trying time.

Richard and I attended a Family Life, "Weekend to Remember" marriage conference. This was pivotal for us, as we began to see and to understand God's plan for marriage and how to communicate in deep and powerful ways. We learned, with open hearts, about the men and women—husbands, wives, and parents—God has called us to be. I remember my husband coming out of the men's breakout session and tearfully sharing: "Our wives are gifts from God. We are held accountable for how we lead them. We will have to answer for this. Did we return our wives better than how we received them?" He wept deeply over this realization.

Since 2008, we have attended many of these conferences and have been big supporters ever since. We send couples each year to the conference, as we believe strongly about the impact. Even if you have a strong marriage, there is something to be gained. Even strong marriages need regular maintenance, focus, and attention to keep it the highest priority, below only our relationship with Christ.

Richard's brother kept asking who *I* was talking to. I needed the same things—wise counsel, support, and leadership. Some women within my family were close to me, and I had a best friend who helped me immensely. They all spoke truth into me and stood by me; they lifted me up and carried me when I could not. How many times did I cry out to my best friend, "I don't understand!"? It's interesting how God works—years later, as she faced her own struggles, having walked this journey with me and witnessing my husband and me overcoming, this gave her the hope to make it through.

Richard's brother and sister-in law told me about a pivotal, long-standing, women's Bible study that met on Thursday mornings. I really didn't want to carve out time for that, but I finally agreed to at least go once and see. Sue Wright, the originator of this Bible study nearly twenty-five years before, shared her testimony and her own broken journey through an awful marriage to an alcoholic husband. She had been invited to a women's

Bible study, and she did not want to go either. She kept with it, though, and God really got hold of her heart.

She began to change, to get her eyes off her husband and onto the Lord, asking what He wanted to change in her own heart. She began to see and understand Jesus's great love for her and about the woman and the wife He called her to be. She began to work on her own hurts and struggles, with a trust building and growing. She learned how to have a personal relationship with Christ by spending time with Him in the Word and so much more. She began to see her husband through Christ's eyes and was able to love him in this way, whether he deserved it or not.

Christ calls us to love and serve our neighbor. Isn't your spouse your closest neighbor? This all starts at home. As Sue began to love him unconditionally and to be transformed by the love of Jesus, her husband couldn't help but notice the changes too. Things worsened for some time before they improved; he fought it hard. I can still hear Sue say, "Remember that in all you do, you are doing it as unto the Lord, whether you want to or not, whether the other person deserves it or not, whether they reciprocate or not." Doesn't this apply to many situations other than marriage, like at work, family relations, or doing something you don't like?

Over time, God did get hold of Sue's husband's heart in a huge way. He accepted the Lord, which slowly transformed him, then their children, and then their entire family. He ended up becoming one of the most influential Bible teachers in the state. They focused their teaching and leading on men and women and restoring marriages. They have saved countless marriages and continue to do so through their recorded messages. Even though they have each passed away now, their legacy lives on.

Funny, after she started speaking, I thought, *Hey, wait a minute. I know this woman's story!* My brother-in-law had given us a set of marriage series CDs. It was on disc, but I could tell it was originally on cassette, which shows how old it was. There were messages such as his testimony, her testimony, forgiveness, communication, how to revive a dull marriage, communication, for men only, for women only, and so on. My husband and I had listened to these and learned a great deal about a godly marriage, biblical principles, and more. They deeply ministered to us, and now, here she was in person. She offered a class called "Loving Your Husband," and

I quickly signed up. This class was pivotal for me in my spiritual growth, and I then became the class assistant for the next few years.

Between this, my daily reading, prayer time, and my now very deep and meaningful conversations with Richard, I have learned much about myself, about my husband, and about the Lord. It was sitting in this Bible study that I first felt the pain and anguish in so many women around me and first heard God's call in my spirit to write a book—my personal journey from brokenness and pain through redemption, grace, healing, and strength. He wanted to use this to help many other women, to take them by the hand and lead them through to the other side.

Reference

1. Moore, Dr. Mark. Weekly sermon. Christ Church of the Valley, Peoria, AZ.

9

FORGIVENESS

When you stand praying, if you hold anything against anyone, forgive
him, so that your Father in heaven may forgive you your sins.
—Mark 11:25 (NIV)

Along the fiery roads I have walked, I've had to learn much about
forgiveness. I wish to share the process I went through so that I could
understand and step into forgiveness for myself. I pray these words help
you do the same. You may be hurting right now, and you need to know
that is normal and OK. Maybe you've never experienced a hurt this deep
before, and you wonder how you can get through it.

Throughout my life, I have experienced great joy and happiness. At my
age, I have also experienced great pain, grief, and anger toward those who
have wronged me, both men and women, and for a variety of reasons. A
lot of these wounds have run deep, yet I have survived and learned how
to overcome, to be the strong and healed person that I am today in Jesus.

So how do you get through it? First, be honest with yourself about your
feelings. Do you feel disappointment, grief, anger, hurt, guilt? Whatever
those feelings are, let them bubble up and out, and be honest about them.
Only then can you begin to purge and process through them. You can't
forgive an offense if you won't let yourself face how angry, hurt, and
betrayed you feel. Stuffing these feelings only will tear you up inside. You
may end up with so much emotional baggage that you become stifled.

I have learned that we often become unable to move on or to maintain
a healthy relationship. In addition, we can make ourselves ill. Many believe
this is where a number of chronic diseases stem from. I believe this is the
root of my IBS (irritable bowel syndrome), which began in childhood. We
can become bitter, and some of us struggle with addictions, seeking to ease

the pain. Bitterness is more than a negative outlook on life; it is destructive and can be physically and emotionally debilitating, not to mention that it can build walls between us and others.

I went through years of these negative effects, of harboring hurts that affected me mentally, emotionally, spiritually, and physically. I realized that I needed to cry out to God and ask for help. He is waiting to help, to comfort, and to pull away the pain. It's important to have people you trust to talk to. The key is for them to be positive, supportive, loving people who keep you uplifted, stand in prayer and faith with you, and give you true, wise, and godly counsel. It is important to watch with whom you surround yourself and to know who is talking in your ear. Worldly advice swims all around you and even makes sense, in all your hurt, but God calls you to His way, which likely may be contrary.

I knew that part of the healing process was about forgiveness. In Mark 11:25, we learn that when we pray, if we hold anything against anyone, we must forgive them so that the Lord may forgive our sins as well.

> For if you forgive men when they sin against you, your heavenly Father will also forgive you. But if you do not forgive others' sins, your Father will not forgive your sins.
>
> —Matthew 6:14–15 NIV)

I asked myself, "How can I *possibly* do this when I have been hurt so deeply?" Did it mean that what someone did was OK? That I would allow it to continue to happen? That I did not hurt? In this, I had to learn the true meaning of forgiveness; it is not what most people assume, and it is not easy. You do it for *yourself*, not for the person who hurt you. Forgiveness brings healing for the forgiver. You forgive for your *own* health; the choice is made to move beyond the offense because you too have been forgiven.

It also helped me immensely to first learn what forgiveness *is not*. Forgiveness is not ignoring, condoning, excusing, or overlooking anything. Extending forgiveness does not mean that what the person did was OK. It is not a free pass for the person to continue the behavior, and it does not ignore your feelings about the situation. It is not simply getting over it or getting past it. Forgiveness does not mean you are letting people off the hook; it just means you are releasing them and turning it over to God. They still must answer to Him, they are still on His hook. Forgiveness does not wipe away your feelings about what happened to you or *take the pain away.* With God's help, that will change over time—*lots of time,* more than you think it should. Often, it happens in stages—at least, it did for me. Forgiveness does not mean there will be reconciliation, nor does it mean that you should leave yourself unprotected.

> When we have been hurt by another person, our tendency is to hang onto our anger and unforgiveness. We wait until the offender circles back to make it right or pay us back. But whether He does or doesn't, God requires us to forgive. He doesn't ask us simply because it benefits the one we forgive, but because it protects our hearts too. The truth is the angst, anger, and hurt of broken relationships will leak. These emotions eventually spill over into our relationships with the most important people in our lives. It will be hard—maybe impossible—to create breathing room in any relationship if our emotional energy is tied up in unforgiveness. So, let this be the push you've been waiting for to finally repair the damage. (Stanley 2017, 137)

When you forgive, others may feel that you don't care enough about what happened to you or your loved ones. When you forgive, it takes *tremendous strength and courage,* even day by day, to not succumb to anger, hurt, hatred, or a need to get even. It is not about what is fair or excusing what happened. Life is never fair. Your forgiveness may not be accepted or acknowledged, but God knows, and it begins to heal your heart; it will keep you from getting pulled farther and farther into a downward spiral. It will also help you to not take out your anger and hurt on others.

Resentment and bitterness tear us up inside, preventing us from moving forward in our lives or in any of our relationships. We must release it to God, and let Him deal with our hearts and with theirs. Forgiveness is not always easy; sometimes, we have to choose it day by day. For me, when the hurt was deep, it sometimes felt like peeling an onion. I would believe I had completely forgiven, and then some new layer would come up to be dealt with, turned over, and released. Trust me; you *do* get to the center of that onion if you don't give up. One day, the emotional charge of the situation *will* pass .You *will* be on the other side of it all, healed and whole, if you do it God's way. The arrows and triggers will come less and less often, and you will know what to do with them when they do.

Even though you choose to forgive others, they still have to answer to God for what they did. They don't get away with anything. If you want forgiveness, you have to grant forgiveness. It may be easier to remember that you need it too. Don't we all want grace in our failings? You are releasing this situation to God so He can deal with it, and you give up your right to punish the one who hurt you. Or continue to beat them over the head with it. Forgiveness is a choice, not a feeling. You *choose* to forgive, even when you don't feel like it. If you wait until you feel like it, it will never happen. The feelings *always* come after you decide to forgive. It is an act of obedience and trust, and then the feelings will follow over time. You can decide to forgive, even though you feel raw, and your heart and head may tell you not to. It is still a decision of the heart. This is what I chose to do, in the power of Christ's strength.

Many fear that forgiveness puts them in a position to be hurt again. God is not asking you to remain a victim or to stay in an unsafe or abusive situation. If this applies to you, please seek help! With certain transgressions, safe boundaries often need to be put in place. Yet Jesus still calls us to forgive; it is the only real way to heal the damage to our own hearts, minds, and souls.

If you are wondering if this means that God forgives them too, it doesn't. God does not forgive until they come to Him in confession, remorse, and *true* repentance. It is not about their feeling bad that they got caught; there has to be a change of heart and actions, a prayer for forgiveness. Repentance is doing an about-face—to turn and go in the opposite direction, not repeating the sin. It is sincere remorse and a heartfelt search for forgiveness. They do not get to this place without the conviction of the Holy Spirit, enabling them to truly see, acknowledge, and demonstrate a sincere and visible change to others. This includes an admission of guilt, an asking for forgiveness, and a promise not to commit it again.

Even as we grow and change in Christ's strength, we may stumble and fall, yet we get back up and keep following him.

Forgiveness between two people does not always mean there will be reconciliation, but there is no hope of it unless true repentance and change take place. This opens the door to the possibility of it. You must have open and clear communication and set protective boundaries. In our case, we established boundaries as mentioned before. We were to always know where the other was at all times. We also realized it was not safe or healthy for either of us to be alone with someone of the opposite sex, let alone try to counsel one. This is something our church also strongly teaches and demonstrates—remove any and all temptation possible. We stopped doing ladies' trips or guys' trips without one another, with rare exceptions. One example was Richard's backpacking through Israel with twelve men, including one of our teaching pastors—an incredible faith opportunity. These were some of the biggies that made a huge difference in restoring our relationship and rebuilding trust.

The person who committed the offense has to rebuild the trust. It is not quick or easy; the person has to earn it and prove it in order to rebuild a new level of intimacy. As I mentioned, it takes a long time, more than you might hope, but stick with it and hang in there. It is possible. My mother-in-law said, "Just watch what God will do. He will give you a love for Richard, and Richard a love for you, that you cannot even imagine." Oh, how badly I wanted that, and no I couldn't really imagine it. Well, that *has* happened and far exceeded any of our wildest dreams—a love so close, so deep, so powerful for each other that it blows our minds at times. God is so good! It does take *both of you* committed to healing a broken marriage, with Christ in the center of your hearts and lives.

In succeeding in these things, our relationship could grow stronger and closer than it ever was before. Our relationship and marriage today can't begin to compare with what it was. Slowly, God knit our hearts together in such a way that we are truly one, as God intended. But we had to do it His way.

What's the point of seeking forgiveness as the offender if you let it touch you only momentarily and then slide back into the same behavior? Forgiveness is useless unless you let it change you for the better.

Forgiveness is powerful, both in receiving it and in granting it; it frees you from the past and helps you to overcome and move forward. It can heal both of you, and you hold the key. Did you know that? Will you choose to forgive and move forward?

In some cases, there cannot be reconciliation between the two people. My abuser is long gone, and he never asked for my forgiveness or acknowledged what he had done. Yet I realized I had to forgive and turn this over to God, as well as including the other men who abused and raped me. When my abuser was on his deathbed, I visited him. It was the most uncomfortable thing for me—the last place I wanted to be. He opened his eyes and seemed so surprised to see me; he looked intently into my eyes. That one look spoke a thousand words to my heart. I could see all the remorse and regret in his eyes, the sorrow. No words were spoken between us audibly, but I believe we both knew. It was like an entire conversation took place in that one look. He passed shortly thereafter. Somehow, there was closure for me, a release.

I had to learn to let go and let God in, to lay it all at his feet. Remember that you do it for yourself, not for them. You let go of the hurt and anger; you cannot move on with your life without it. Unforgiveness ties God's hands from working in your life and from bringing you peace and healing your broken heart.

How do you do this? Ask God for help; it is possible. Pour your heart and your hurts out to him. Ask Him to help you forgive. "Lord, I don't know how to forgive. Please help me." You decide, knowing that you cannot do it without His strength. As I mentioned, it is a choice before you feel like it. Ask God to help you with your feelings and emotions. He knows your emotions have great power over you.

I hear Sue Wright again saying, "Sometimes you need to tell your feelers to take a hike!" Oh, I have said this many times!

Remember that you're the only one who can keep you from being the person God created you to be. Choose to grow in Christ and forgive those around you, extending grace. Seek unity and create an environment in which your family can thrive. Know that you will still have bad days— more so in the beginning—but keep putting one foot in front of the other toward Christ, and those days will become fewer and fewer.

Remember that you *can* control what you choose to think about. Take your thoughts captive. Say, "*No*, I have already forgiven that. I'm not going to go there." Focus on what is good, and working, and right. What can you be thankful for? Don't be too hard on yourself; healing and forgiveness is a process. It takes time to deal with all of those emotions and to grieve. Don't stuff these things; it will only make you sick. Let them out, but control your thought life. Don't let it run away with you. For some things, it may take years to fully experience the healing of forgiveness. Stick with it; forgiveness is a decision to trust that God knows more than you and that forgiving the person will heal your heart. I forgave because I trusted that God loves me and that He would never tell me to do something that wasn't good for me. I wanted to heal. I wanted to be whole.

Ephesians 4:26 says to be angry and sin not. Anger in itself is not sin. It's what we do with our anger that makes it sinful. I find it helpful to express the anger in a letter to the person who offended me, which I don't send. This helps me understand what God is asking me to forgive, specifically, and why. Burning the letter, as a way of letting go, can be very freeing, or you can simply hit delete.

Confess your own sins. How have you allowed this unforgiveness to influence you? Have you been angry at God? Have you become afraid to live and to love well? Have you been afraid to trust? Have you treated others poorly because of it? Do you use it as a weapon? I needed to honestly admit and repent my own responsibility in the situation, regardless of the percentage of my responsibility. You may think you have no fault or that your percentage of responsibility may be less than it really is. Ask God what He wants you to learn about yourself in this situation. Then be open to receiving, repenting, and releasing these heart attitudes. Commit to forgiveness. It's time to let God do what only He can do; let Him cleanse places in your heart and in your soul that you can never reach in your own strength. Trust God, and watch Him set you free!

Reference

1. Stanley, Sandra. 2017. *Breathing Room: A 28-Day Devotional for Women*. Georgia, USA: North Point Ministries.

10

BATTLING FEAR AND WORRY

When you pass through the waters, I will be with you: and through the rivers, they shall not overwhelm you: when you walk through the fire you shall not be burned, and the flame shall not consume you.
—Isaiah 43:2 (ESV)

Know that the arrows and triggers will come. That song, this person, that place—and believe it or not, there is an enemy, and he wants to keep you from a relationship with God and from reconciling your relationship with the one who hurt you. But you are not left alone here. God gives you the tools to defend and fight your battles. Remember that it's important to control your mind, your thoughts, and what you choose to dwell on. For me, this is getting into prayer, calling a godly mentor for wise counsel (today, that is most often my husband), listening to faith music, shifting to a heart space of gratitude, journaling, getting in the Bible, and listening to God speak to me.

When all of this was going on, I felt I could not face anyone at our company. I was too fearful of judgment and humiliation. I believed they could not understand why I was doing what I was. I was afraid to face people; it took so much out of me.

My mom told me, "You have always been so strong and so bold. How are you letting this fear control you now?" Just after she said that, I turned on the radio, and a song spoke right into that truth again. God was showing me—through my mom and through the song—that I needed to face my fear. I scheduled lunch with Richard and met at the office to pick him up and see everyone. It was extremely awkward for me. I am sure it was for them too but not nearly like what I feared. It did not take long for all of that to pass away. Amen

The Lord is my light and my salvation, whom shall I fear?
The Lord is the stronghold of my life, of whom shall I be
afraid?

—Psalm 27:1 (ESV)

Pastor Ashley Wooldridge, senior pastor of Christ Church of the
Valley, once said, "Fear can put blinders on seeing God clearly ... Often
the thing God wants you to do and the place He wants you to go are
exactly opposite of what fear wants. Run from your fear and you might
be running from your future. What you fear the most is often where you
trust God the least."

I come from a long line of worriers, and I'm sorry to say that I have
passed it on to my daughters. It's a tough habit to break. Anxiety can run
in the family too. I hate to admit to being stressed or having an anxious
heart. Somehow, saying I have an "anxious heart" sounds better to me.
I saw how silly that looked as I typed those words here, as if calling it
something different makes it better somehow. Many say that we learn the
most about ourselves and grow when we write.

A few months ago, I was feeling anxious but could not place exactly
why. Was I worried about my brother, my daughter's job struggles in LA,
looming art shows, hanging my art at the museum? *What is it?* I thought.
What is going on with me? This uneasy feeling continued for days, even at
the cabin, preparing to go to the lake with a group. Why was I so anxious?
Tossing and turning at night, I could not sleep. Finally, I got up and
grabbed my Bible, journal, and pen. I was going to look up every verse I
could find on worry and fear and write them down. Here are some of those
that impacted me the most.

Fear of man shall prove to be a snare, but whoever trusts
in the Lord is kept safe.

—Proverbs 29:25 (NIV)

This is the verse that got me out the door, choosing to fear no man or
woman any longer. The footnote in my *NIV Study Bible* says that fear of
man can hamper everything you do. In extreme forms, it can make you

afraid to leave your home. By contrast, fear of God (meaning reverence, awe, respect, trust) is liberating.

> Do not be anxious about anything, but in every situation, by prayer and petition, with thanksgiving, present your requests to God.
>
> —Philippians 4:6 (NIV)

This is one of my all-time favorite life verses, and I have it memorized. I also have it posted on the wall, where I often will see it. Over and over again, this verse helps to recenter me, bringing peace where there was none and washing away my anxiety.

> Finally, brothers and sisters, whatever is true, whatever is noble, whatever is right, whatever is pure, whatever is lovely, whatever is admirable—if anything is excellent or praiseworthy—think about such things.
>
> —Philippians 4:8 (NIV)

Here I see how I am to take my thoughts captive and make them obedient to Christ. You do have control over what you choose to dwell on. It is important to retrain your way of thinking and what you choose to spend your time dwelling on. This is a practice, a discipline, replacing a bad habit for a good one.

> Peace I leave with you, my peace I give you. Do not let your hearts be troubled and do not be afraid.
>
> —John 14:27 (NIV)

Ah, there it is—God's promise.

"Can any one of you by worrying add a single hour to your life?"

—Matthew 6:27 (NIV)

How much of what I worry about *ever* comes to pass?

But seek first His kingdom and His righteousness, and all these things will be given to you as well. Therefore, do not worry about tomorrow, for tomorrow will worry about itself. Each day has enough trouble of its own.

—Matthew 6:33–34 (NIV)

NIV footnote:

Planning for tomorrow is time well spent, worrying about tomorrow is time wasted. The negative effects of worry damage health, cause the object of your worry to consume your thoughts, negatively affect how you treat others, disrupt productivity, and reduce our ability to trust God.

Boy, isn't that the truth! I must rest in the present, taking God's outstretched hand as He walks me through each day. Worry created a downward spiral that dragged me down a rabbit hole, time and time again. I must seek God daily and choose to spend time with him.

Do not worry about what to say or how to say it. At that time you will be given what to say, for it will not be you speaking but the Spirit of our Father speaking through you.

—Matthew 10:19–20 (NIV)

Amen. I have prayed the above verse many times when I have needed to have a difficult conversation or before speaking to a large group. I love this promise and have found it to be true in my own life. I trust that God will give me the right words to say when I need to say them.

The footnote on Exodus 4:1 of my *NIV Study Bible* is:

> We often build up events in our minds and then panic over what might go wrong. God does not ask us to go where He has not provided the means to help. Go where He leads, trusting Him to supply courage, confidence, and the resources at the right moment.

I love this. I feel my heart calming already, my breathing deepens, the tight squeeze releasing within, as the promises go on.

> Don't be afraid, stand firm, and you will see the deliverance that Lord will bring you today … the Lord will fight for you, you need only be still.
>
> —Exodus 14:13–14 (NIV)

> The Lord is my light and my salvation, whom shall I fear. The Lord is the stronghold of my life, of whom shall I be afraid.
>
> —Psalm 27:1 (NIV)

> For the Spirit God gave us does not make us timid, but gives us power, love and self-discipline.
>
> —2 Timothy 1:7 (NIV)

The way to bring peace to a troubled heart is to trust in God's promises and to do what He says.

After finishing this exercise, I was able to sleep peacefully and soundly, thanking God. Upon waking and in the days that followed, the oppression lifted. What a beautiful thing! *Thank you, Lord, for reminding me of your promises once again.* How easily I can forget—why is that? I think it's because I get my eyes off God and back onto my problems or fears.

As I walk this great unknown, Questions come and
questions go. Was their purpose for the pain?
Did I cry these tears in vain?
I don't want to live in fear
I want to trust that You are near …
I have this hope
In the depth of my soul …
You're with me and You won't let go
—"I Have This Hope" by Tenth Avenue North

Put Your Armor On!

I have found another critical part of protecting my mind, heart, and
spirit is by putting my armor on daily. God has given us these offensive and
defensive tools and weapons, along with the call to prayer to stay protected.
My husband and I have a prayer we say every morning together, putting
God's armor on. The prayer is based on the following scripture:

Finally, be strong in the Lord and in His mighty power.
Put on the full armor of God, so that you can take your
stand against the devil's schemes. For our struggle is not
against flesh and blood, but against the rulers, against
the authorities, against the powers of this dark world and
against the spiritual forces of evil in the heavenly realms.
Therefore, put on the full armor of God, so that when the
day of evil comes, you may be able to stand your ground,
and after you have done everything, to stand. Stand firm
then, with the belt of truth buckled around your waist,
with the breastplate of righteousness in place, and with
your feet fitted with the readiness that comes from the
gospel of peace. In addition to all this, take up the shield
of faith, with which you can extinguish all the flaming
arrows of the evil one. Take the helmet of salvation and
the sword of the Spirit, which is the word of God. And
pray in the Spirit on all occasions with all kinds of prayers

and requests. With this in mind, be alert and always keep on praying for all the Lord's people.

—Ephesians 6:10–18 (NIV)

Richard and I have found there is so much power in our prayer. We sure can tell a difference between when we are praying it and when we are not. If you feel under attack, put your armor on! This is our prayer we created based on this verse:

"Father, I come before you, putting on the armor of God in faith, starting with the shoes of peace, standing firm in all situations; the belt of truth, filling me with wisdom and discernment; then the breastplate of righteousness, guarding my heart and emotions. Next, the helmet of salvation, protecting my mind and my thoughts. Next, the shield of faith, with which I deflect *all* of Satan's fiery arrows; and last, the sword of the Spirit, your Word, Father, wielded in offense and in defense. In your name I pray, amen."

The Power of Prayer

Never forget the power of prayer to move in a situation. I've seen answers to prayers over and over again. Some of these prayers were answered as I wanted; some were not answered how or when I wanted, but God did move in those situations, and I saw His handiwork. I am still waiting for the answers to others but trust that He is moving behind the scenes. Sometimes, prayers don't seem to be answered, yet God uses those situations to come alongside you, perhaps, and to be a light to another going through similar situations.

Just after praying in the night over my fears with these verses, I started reading the book *Fervent* by Priscilla Shirer. What a mighty, powerful book on prayer, directed primarily to women. I highly recommend it. After reading it, I asked Richard to read it with me. He agreed, and we read it aloud together. He found much power in this reading about prayer life and applying it. In *Fervent*, Shirer calls us to write out our prayers, with scriptural promises, and post them where we can see then and pray over each one daily. "You write your prayers ... so that you won't forget," she says.

> Through intentional, deliberate, strategic prayers, you grab hold of Jesus and everything He has already done on your behalf.
>
> Nothing—nothing—is too far gone that God cannot resurrect it ... prayer, fervent, strategic prayer, can change things. Even unchangeable things. Even things as unchangeable as real-life scenes from your past—what you did, what you didn't do, why you did it, why you didn't. No, prayer doesn't wipe them all away, doesn't pretend they never happened. And no, it doesn't remove every natural, logical consequence from playing itself out. But just as God says to the ocean waves, "Thus far you shall come, but no farther" —Job 38:11 (NIV).
>
> He has given us prayer to raise us up above the sea level of Satan's assault from our past.
>
> Through prayer you'll not only be able to defend yourself from incoming sniper fire, but through almighty God will be able to push into enemy territory and take ... stuff ... back! (2016, 7, 12, 95)

Oh, I love this—*that's enough*. I have had it. I will no longer let these situations control me, my thoughts, my actions, or my emotions. I'm taking a stand. Will you?

After I finished reading *Fervent*, we were preparing to go to Washington, DC, for Mary Jane's son's wedding; he is like a son to us. It would be a long flight, so I was digging through my bookshelf for something to read. A book came to mind that another great friend had given me a year or so before, but I hadn't read yet—*The Circle Maker* by Mark Batterson. I only remembered her saying it was *so* good. I threw it in my bag and headed for the airport.

On the plane, I settled in and began to read; it was another book on prayer. *Interesting*, I thought. *Working on me here, Lord? Apparently.* This is where it got bizarre. I soon learned Batterson's book was set in DC, just where we were going, and it was about his journey of starting his church on Capitol Hill. *What are the odds?* I thought. *He talks of walking all the streets we will soon walk, of many of the places we will be visiting.*

Funny—my friend's son and his bride talked to us about an incredible coffee shop they wanted to take us to that was owned by Christians. They were so excited to share it with us. On the flight home, I learned that coffee shop, Ebenezer's, was owned and was started by Mark Batterson and his church as an outreach. Again, I was blown away by how God moves. This book had been on my shelf for over a year, and now I began reading it? Wow! The timing was simply uncanny. Of course, I shared this with Mary Jane, and she immediately bought the book for herself and for her son too.

Mark Batterson talks about the "Legend of the Circle Maker":

> It was the first century BC and a devastating drought threatened to destroy a generation, the generation before Jesus. The last of the Jewish Prophets had died off nearly four centuries before. Miracles were a distant memory and they seemed like false memory. And God was nowhere to be heard. But there was one man, an eccentric sage who lived outside the walls of Jerusalem, who dared to pray anyway. His name was Honi. And even if people could no longer hear God, he believed God could hear them.

> When the rain is plentiful it is an afterthought, during a drought it is the only thought. And Honi was their only hope … With a six-foot staff in his hand, Honi began to turn like a math compass. His circular movement was rhythmical and methodical … Honi stood in the circle he had drawn. Then he dropped to his knees and raised his hands to Heaven. With the authority of the prophet Elijah, who called down fire from Heaven, Honi called down the rain. "Lord of the universe, I swear before your great name that I will not move from this circle until You have shown mercy upon your children." … It was not just

the volume of his voice but the authority of his tone, not even a hint of doubt. As his prayer ascended, raindrops descended to the earth.

Honi continued to pray, and it rained so much that flooding occurred.

The prayer that saved the generation was deemed one of the most significant prayers in the history of Israel. (Batterson, 2016, 11-13)

Throughout his book, Batterson uses the analogy of praying this powerfully in our own lives—praying prayer circles around our circumstances and the people we love.

Bold prayers honor God and God honors bold prayers ... There is nothing God honors more than keeping promises, answering prayers, performing miracles, and fulfilling dreams. That is who He is, that is what He does.

Who you become is determined by how you pray ... drawing circles starts with discerning what God wants and what God wills.

He goes onto say, "You never know how or when God will answer, but I promise you this: He will answer."

This is so true; there is unbelievable power in prayer. I have experienced this time and time again. God moves mountains, though not always the way you think He should and not in your timing but in His. It's critical to develop your prayer life, to spend time with Him in this way. Prayer has been very important to me in my faith journey. Clearly, with these two powerful books on prayer, He was wanting to bring my prayer life to the next level—maybe even preparing me for something.

Batterson also shares that our prayers never die; they are always out there working. *I love that!* I began to visualize taking my staff and carving a circle around my husband, daughters, brother, parents, and anyone or anything else God led me to. In doing so, I would cover each of them in diligent and relentless prayer, regularly. He asks, "What is your Jericho?

What walls do you need to fall and keep circling until they do?" Another great visual for me—in prayer and promise to keep circling until they do.

Thank you, Jesus, for continuing to show me who You want me to pray for right now—and for what.

When you pray, it's important to pray specifically, not vaguely, and to rest on God's promises for each. What is it that you want Him to do in those situations? Don't give up when you don't see results. Prayer is about consistency, diligence, fervent prayer, and praying through, even when things seem to get tougher, and you don't see God moving. The mountain before you often gets steeper or more treacherous before your biggest breakthrough, before your miracle. Don't give up; don't give in. Trust that God is in control and can see so much more that you ever could. His plan is best and so is His timing.

I can't tell you how many times He has exceeded what I was praying for in such a powerful way and, at times, so differently than I pictured. He is not limited by our limited understanding of space or time. Pray big dreams—he loves that. At some time, we then stop praying for it and start praising Him for it, for answers to our prayers, thanking Him for bringing us though in a mighty way.

Dr. Don Wilson, founding pastor of Christ Church of the Valley, has said, "Sorry looks back, worry looks around, faith looks ahead." How true this is.

Know that, sometimes, God's answers are *no* or *not yet*. But that is only because He has something better for us. We wait upon the Lord in expectation, knowing He has our best interests at heart. He can be trusted. We are all part of a greater plan at work, all for His glory.

> And if you have the faith to dream big, pray hard, and think long, there is nothing God loves more than proving His faithfulness ... those bottled prayers God will unseal in God's time, in God's way, He will answer somewhere, sometime, somehow. All you have to do is keep circling."
> (Batterson 2016)

References

1. Batterson, Mark. 2016. *The Circle Maker: Praying Circles around Your Biggest Fears.* Grand Rapids, MI: Zondervan.
2. Wilson, Don. Weekly sermon. Christ Church of the Valley, Peoria, AZ.
3. Woolridge, Pastor Ashley. Weekly sermon. Christ Church of the Valley, Peoria, AZ.
4. Shirer, Priscilla Evans. 2016. *Fervent: A Woman's Battle Plan for Serious, Specific, and Strategic Prayer.* Nashville, TN: B & H Publishing Group.

11

What I Learned about Myself

Lord, search my heart, and root out anything that does not belong.

Throughout my time at Valley West Women's Bible Study, professional counseling, prayer, mentoring, spending time in my Bible, and journaling—I have learned much. My marriage implosion *finally* had me fully surrender to Christ and invite Him all the way in. I put Him at the center of my life and my marriage. I've mentioned how we lived "one foot in and one foot out" for such a long time. Clearly, my way was not working. *Let's do this your way, Lord.*

Surrender sounds like defeat to many. This kind of surrender, however, is completely different. It is *so* freeing, a liberation. It's like a gigantic boulder is removed from your shoulders. Such a burden lifts as we lay it all at God's feet. It was never ours to carry in the first place.

> Come to me, all you who are weary and burdened, and I
> will give you rest.
>
> —Matthew 11:28 (NIV)

Surrender is trusting in Jesus, Abba Father, completely, knowing He loves me fully and has my own best interest in mind.

> He will never leave you or forsake you.
>
> —Deuteronomy 31:6 (NIV)

God knows all and sees all, far more than I could ever comprehend. He knows the way far better than I do. I will choose to follow Him. I have seen for myself how He has brought me through *every* single trial in my life, how He has shown up when I needed Him the most, how He is always there. I hear Him speak to me in many ways, knowing full well it is Him. Nothing is too big or too small for Him to be concerned about. He is intimately involved and wishes me to seek Him in *all* things, large and small.

For the word of God will never fail.

—Luke 1:37 (NLT))

Not even saving my marriage was too difficult for Jesus.

For I am the Lord your God, who takes ahold of your right hand and says to you, do not fear, I will help you.

—Isaiah 41:13 (NIV)

One of the most important things I had to learn was to get my eyes off of my husband and my circumstances and onto Christ. I needed to stop worrying about what Richard was or was not doing, his faith journey. I needed to leave that to God (and pray without ceasing). I needed to turn inward and take a hard look at myself. What did God want to show me about the state of my own heart, about the lies I had believed, and about my responsibility in the state of my marriage? We all play a part. I am not condoning my husband's actions, but we must take ownership for our own issues and responsibility in the state of our marriages, our circumstances. No matter how small we might think our responsibility is, we must face it and see how God wants to grow and change us to be all He created us to be. What garbage is in my heart that needs to be rooted out, disposed of, and healed? It's interesting how we always seem to feel our portion is smaller than it really is.

I realized that I too had a God-shaped hole in my heart, and I was trying to fill it with many things, mainly my husband. I based my happiness or feelings of security on what he was doing or not doing, how he was acting and responding. This became a roller coaster.

Listen, you cannot expect another person to be responsible for your own happiness or contentedness. This puts pressure on the other person that he or she can never stand up under. No husband, or anyone else for that matter, will ever be able to meet all of your needs. Every person in every relationship you have will let you down sometimes. None of us is perfect; we all make mistakes; we all stumble and fall, myself included. How many mistakes and regrets have I had? So many.

> It is a foolish woman who expects her husband to be to her what only Jesus Christ himself can be: always ready to forgive, totally understanding, unendingly patient, invariably tender and loving, unfailing in every area, anticipating every need, and making more than adequate provision. Such expectations put a man under an impossible strain. (Graham 1988, 74)

What a powerful passage—this really helped to reshape my thoughts and my heart. Only Christ can fill this place in me, bringing wholeness, healing, joy, peace, and contentedness. I cannot rely on anyone or anything to make me happy.

> Whom have I in heaven but you. And earth has nothing I desire besides you. My flesh and my heart may fail, but God is the strength of my heart and my portion forever.
>
> —Psalm 73:25–26 (NIV)

> My soul finds rest in God alone; my salvation comes from Him. He alone is my rock and my salvation.
>
> —Psalm 62:1–2 (NIV)

> All we need to live as Christians, no matter what our circumstances, is the security of His love and the significance of participation in His purpose. We must

never claim that our relationships with others do not deeply affect us: they do. But Christ's resources are enough to keep us going. (Crabb 2013, p. 119)

There Is No Such Thing as Control, Let Go

I learned from all the damage and arrows and my feeling so out of control in situations where I was taken advantage of that I *had* to be in control. Isn't that what we tend to do when we've been hurt—try to control everything and everyone around us so we cannot be hurt again? We build walls around our hearts. My journey through childhood traumas, to an extreme diagnosis, to relational problems, to natural disasters has taught me that I really have no control at all. It was an illusion. The more I tried to hold on tight and control my circumstances, the more they seemed to slip away, like grains of sand through a closing fist. I tried to control my husband's actions, what he said or didn't say, and how others perceived him. I couldn't make my husband love me; I can't make my adult kids do anything they don't want to do. Can you imagine trying to live up to such pressure?

I would fall into mothering Richard and talking down to him. Of course, I didn't see it that way; I saw it as *helping*. I had to learn that I am not my husband's Holy Spirit, nor am I his mother. Who wants to be married to their mother anyway?

Arizona Pastor, Tom Shrader, once spoke at our women's Bible study and asked, "Would you want to come home to *you*?" He also had said that who you are at home is who you are—ouch. I had to finally lay all of this down—my own complete surrender to the Lord.

Jesus, I trust you. Come fully and completely into my heart. Lead and guide me in your ways. Show me what you would have me say and do.

For my thoughts are not your thoughts, neither are your ways my ways, declares the Lord.

—Isaiah 55:8 (NIV)

I must keep my focus on Christ, and He will bring true peace into my heart and mind. I must keep my eyes off my husband and lay him at the feet of Jesus. I must let Jesus work on my husband and family, trust in that process, and love them unconditionally, just as I trust God is working on me too.

Don't Sweat the Small Stuff

Richard would always say, "Don't sweat the small stuff." How true that is. Over time, so many things about your spouse or kids can drive you out of your mind, like putting dishes in the sink without rinsing them, leaving socks in a ball inside out, or misusing that *same* word over and over again. I admit that has been a tough one for me. How about the trail of messes behind your kids? I had to ask myself, *Is any of this really that important?* I'm not saying you should never say anything. There is a time and a place, in love, to share how certain actions might make you feel. There are also times when it is better to choose your battles wisely, and let the small stuff slide. Shift your heart space to one of gratitude. These things are all signs that loved ones are in our lives. Just ask the widow or the mother who has lost a child if she wouldn't give anything to have those little irritating things back again. What can you be thankful for about your spouse, your kids? I choose to focus on these things. Am I creating a peaceful haven for my family to come home to, or am I too wrapped up in to-do lists and these irritations?

And how many things do we do that drive our families up the walls? How about that my phone is dead half the time when Richard needs to reach me, or that I leave my phone and purse many places they do not belong? What about how accident-prone I am or not having my medication on me when I need it. These things drive him wild, and truth be told, they drive me wild too. Don't I want grace for these things as well?

As I began to learn that it is Christ who meets all my needs, this took the pressure off those around me. It helped me to see them through the eyes of grace. I prayed constantly—and do even now—to see others through Christ's eyes. This helped me to learn, through humbleness and gentleness, to serve my husband and children and others, not out of obligation but out of love. I learned I must humble myself and look to the needs of my husband and others. How can I meet his needs and lift him up? This humility is not about knocking yourself down but taking the primary focus off yourself and shifting it to others. It is thinking about yourself less and others more. Ask yourself, "How may I help, encourage, lift up?"

I learned not to anxious but to rest in Christ, in faith and prayer, about my marriage. I learned to let the Lord lead me, even if it was uncomfortable, even if there were times I didn't feel like it. As I stayed in God's undeniable and unconditional love, I was better able to love and serve my husband and others without expectation. I began to truly understand the greatest commandment for myself:

> Love the Lord your God with all your heart and with all your soul and with all your mind and with all your strength. The second is this: Love your neighbor as yourself. There is no commandment greater than these.
>
> —Mark 12:30–31 (NIV)

Do you realize that your closest neighbor is your spouse, your children? Loving your neighbor truly starts at home. Jesus did not say, if they deserve it, if they love me back, if they believe like me, if they will ever believe like me. He said to love your neighbor as yourself. This means to love them as Christ loves us, to serve them as unto the Lord.

Women Have So Much Power

Women have so much power in their homes. Are you wielding it for good or for bad? Are you building up or tearing down? Convicting right? Well it was for me.

> The wise woman builds her house, but with her own hands the foolish one tears hers down.
>
> —Proverbs 14:1 (NIV)

> By wisdom, a house is built, and through understanding
> it is established. Through knowledge its rooms are filled
> with rare and beautiful treasures.
>
> —Proverbs 24:3–4 (NIV)

I learned I really do set the tone in the home. Am I creating a place for my husband and children where they feel encouraged and cherished, safe and secure, and loved unconditionally? Am I building my home in wisdom?

I remember too many times when I frustrated my family just before parties and holiday gatherings. I was stressed and pressured, barking out last-minute orders, like a drill sergeant, so everything would be perfect when guests arrived. How perfect could it be when I caused my husband and daughters so much strife? I am very thankful to have let this go, for the most part. So what if everything is not in its place? Am I being a Martha or a Mary in this situation? Jesus came to their home and spoke. Mary stayed at his feet to absorb everything He had to say. Martha was running around, stressed, trying to be the best hostess and take care of everything. She even complained to Jesus and asked Him to make Mary help her. Jesus said Mary has chosen what was best and He would not take it from her. Are not family and friends, even strangers, more important than having everything in order? There is much less self-inflicted pressure now and so much more laughter and joy.

A Time to Play

How many years was I so serious, not even knowing how to be playful, not feeling free to laugh and play? My husband was just the opposite. He instilled in the girls such a playful silliness; I love it. He has taught me much; they have taught me much—to laugh more and lighten up, to not be so serious, to be more adventurous and playful. I am so grateful for this. God knew just what I needed in them.

I want to laugh at the days to come. Help me to always see the laughs, the jokes, the twinkle in their eyes, and to join in freely and regularly myself, Lord.

What about My Words?

I needed to look at how I was speaking to my family. I still do. Why do we tend to bark at the ones we love when we feel under pressure? What did I learn growing up about tone of voice and harsh words? Did they not sting me deeply? Why, then, would I do the same thing? Habits learned are tough to break. It takes intentionality and determination, prayer, and the power of Christ to break the cycle, to put a stake in the ground. Am I perfect in this? Certainly not! Just ask my family. But praise God that He loves me too much to leave me where I am. He is constantly working on my heart, my mind, *and* my mouth.

With Christ on my mind, first and always each day, I can focus on Him and his Word, rather than act and react selfishly or carelessly. I also must remember to not interrupt or correct. We try to finish each other's sentences way too much; I still struggle with this today. I realize this dishonors the person who is speaking, showing them that what they have to say is not important. It also means we are poor listeners when we interrupt. Lord, help me to genuinely listen and be present in the moment, without thinking about what I am going to say next. Help me to seek and trust the Holy Spirit to give me the right words to say at the right time and to put a hand over my mouth when I should not speak (Holy Duct Tape!).

How am I doing? Well, just last night, Richard and I got into it. We had shared dinner with his parents. He was describing his journey through Jerusalem (he'd just returned), and I kept interjecting comments, *helping* him tell his story. I was excited for him and spoke up, interrupting, pointing out things I thought he should share.

On the drive home, he seemed not himself. When I asked him if something was wrong, he said he felt I had been correcting him or trying to have him tell it the way *I* wanted him to. He was not happy. What was I doing? I truly had meant nothing by it and thought I was actually helping. It didn't matter, though; what mattered was how *he* felt about it.

I apologized, yet it was a long, silent ride home. I kept thinking, *This is exactly what I am writing about.* Did he feel honored? No. Why did I feel the need to interrupt and speak for him? Why do I forget at times—even now? Argh! Sometimes old habits die hard. Or was it a form of spiritual attack, knowing I am writing on this right now. Or was God showing me my heart and that there was still more to be rid of?

After we were home for a while, I started to wonder if we would be going to bed upset, something we made a point to not do anymore. Then he walked up to me, kissed me gently—once, twice, three times—and I knew without words. Grace. Amen.

> Do not let any unwholesome talk come out of your mouths, but only what is helpful for building others up according to their needs, that it may benefit those who listen ... Be kind and compassionate to one another, forgiving each other, just as in Christ God forgave you.
>
> —Ephesians 4:29, 32 (NIV)

> The words of the reckless pierce like swords, but the tongue of the wise brings healing.
>
> —Proverbs 12:18 (NIV)

> When there are many words, transgression is unavoidable, but he who restrains his lips is wise.
>
> —Proverbs 10:19 (NASB)

> A gentle answer turns away wrath, but a harsh word stirs up anger.
>
> —Proverbs 15:1 (NIV)

> I have found the above words to be true; it's hard to argue in a whisper.

> The tongue has the power of life and death.
>
> —Proverbs 18:21 (NIV)

For the mouth speaks out of that which fills the heart.

—Matthew 12:34 (NIV)

What is the state of my heart? I had to genuinely take a hard look at this and make some changes. I think it's important to constantly ask, "Lord, search my heart, and root out anything that does not belong."

> Everyone should be quick to listen, slow to speak and slow to become angry, because human anger does not produce the righteousness that God desires.

—James 1:19–20 (NIV)

Why is it so hard for me to be quick to listen and slow to speak? Lord, teach me to be a better listener. Break the cycle of feeling like I need to talk all the time and the need to be right.

> Do not merely listen to the word, and so deceive yourselves. Do what it says. Anyone who listens to the word but does not do what it says is like someone who looks at his face in a mirror and, after looking at himself, goes away and immediately forgets what he looks like. But whoever looks intently into the perfect law that gives freedom and continues in it—not forgetting what they have heard but doing it—they will be blessed in what they do. Those who consider themselves religious and yet do not keep a tight rein on their tongues deceive themselves, and their religion is worthless.

—James 1:22–26 (NIV)

What of My Own Actions Contributed to the State of my Marriage?

I spent time in reflection, shortly after our marriage went up in flames, realizing I needed to analyze my own actions, especially while under the influence of alcohol. I was a happy drunk and a silly one, but I was also a flirty one. I drank too much in social situations and behaved poorly. With new eyes, I could see not only how dangerous this and the situations in which I found myself were; I had been clueless. I learned more about how men are wired and how they think. I recognized how dishonoring this was to my husband. Why was I like this? I think the alcohol amplified my need for approval, especially from the opposite sex. I constantly needed validation that I was accepted, loved, pretty, wanted, and so on. Often, deep down in a woman's soul, she cries out, *Am I loved? Am I safe? Am I beautiful? Am I enough?* And then Jesus showed me who I really was. It took time for me to see how Jesus really saw me—beloved and wonderfully and fearfully made.

> For You created my inmost being; You knit me together in my mother's womb. I praise you because I am fearfully and wonderfully made; your works are wonderful; I know that full well. My frame was not hidden from You when I was made in the secret place, when I was woven together in the depths of the earth. Your eyes saw my unformed body; all the days ordained for me were written in your book before one of them came to be. How precious to me are Your thoughts, how vast is the sum of them! Were I to count them, they would outnumber the grains of sand— when I awake, I am still with You.
>
> —Psalm 139:13–18 (NIV)

Jesus showed me how fervently He loves me. He knew me before I was born, and I was chosen. He had a plan and purpose for me, and I am safe in him, wholly loved, wholly desired. I heard: *Child of mine, abide in me—an audience of one. Come to me, all who are weary, and I will give you rest.* I love when He calls me *child*, and I'm thankful to hear it often when I spend time with him.

Where Was Jesus?

I came to realize that Jesus was there through everything I went through, even the most horrid things. I realized this, not just through the teachings I was studying but through the Holy Spirit, Jesus revealed this to me. He wept passionately with me as these things happened. He held me and carried me when I could not carry myself, like "Footprints in the Sand." Many times, He has intervened in my life through prayer and changed situations in a dramatic way. But sometimes, He does not seem to directly intervene to stop something from happening.

People ask all the time, "Where was God in all this? Why didn't He stop it?" I cannot fully answer the questions as to why, but I asked a lot of those same questions. Bad things happen all the time. Let's face it; we live in a fallen world. We were all given free will. Sometimes, things happen because of another's poor choices that affect us. Sometimes, it is our own poor choices and their consequences. Sometimes, God disciplines us, as a loving father or mother would, to teach and to train. And sometimes, there is a greater plan in place that we may not fully understand—at least, not yet—until we can look back. Who knows why He did not intervene to stop some of my traumas?

I don't believe God makes bad things happen to me, but I do know that everything filters through His hands. He is aware of these things and may choose, for His own purposes, to stop them—or not. I *know* He brings me through, holds my hand, and "is a lamp for my feet, and a light on my path" —Psalm 119:105 (NIV).

> I have told you these things, so that in me you may have peace. In this world you will have trouble. But take heart! I have overcome the world.
>
> —John 16:33 (NLT)

He can and will bring something good out of each trial I endure and overcome—if I let him.

Maybe it is simply to come alongside others who are struggling through the same thing I endured. I can walk with them and bring them hope, as others did for me. Maybe my story will bring hope and healing to others. Many times, I see God moving in profound ways. It often takes getting through it and looking back to recognize these things. Who knew I would step out in faith and courage and write a book? I pray constantly that my journey brings light, encouragement, and hope. I pray for the courage to be transparent and to reveal these vulnerable trials, and I pray that my loved ones and I are not judged.

You too can make it to the other side. You too can be filled with joy and peace, strength and wisdom. This too shall pass. As the seasons change, the leaves fall; winter comes, then the promise of spring and rebirth, into the warmth of summer. One season after another.

Abba Father

For many, it can be difficult to see almighty God as a loving Father; intimately, Abba Father (Daddy). This is especially the case if you did not experience your natural father this way or he was absent, or if men took advantage of you or hurt you. For me, it was a gradual process of learning to trust a little at a time and then seeing God prove His faithfulness and great love for me. I saw God move in my situations, leading and guiding me. He was and is always there, proving himself trustworthy.

Thankfully, I know Him intimately now. And what a beautiful place this is! I wish this for you more than anything. The beauty of it all is almost indescribable—to truly know Him as Abba Father, fully trustworthy, always there, and to be fully known by him. How did I get here? By spending time with him—in His Word, through prayer, and through journaling.

How do you develop a close relationship with anyone? By spending consistent quality time with them, making them a priority, and being intentional. A relationship with our heavenly Father is much the same.

Submission

I learned about submission and what it truly means and does not mean. I must admit that I had a real problem with this. I thought, *I will submit to no man!* I would not have it in my wedding vows, as I saw it derogatory—him over me; me below. And men often misuse scripture in this way, instituting a dictatorship and telling their wives what to do. This is *not* what Christ intended, not even close.

Women are not to be treated as doormats and walked over. Submission doesn't mean to keep silent when they have something important to say; it is not being less than, less important, or unequal to. Wives are joint heirs with their husbands, made in the image of Christ. Submission is an attitude of the heart, a willful decision to honor God's role by following the husband's leadership. He is called to be the leader of the family, and with that comes great responsibility *and* accountability. Christ calls husbands to servant leadership, honoring and serving their wives as they lead and sacrifice for them and their family.

Wives are called to be their husbands' helpmates and to give them wise counsel. Wives see, understand, and discern things that their husbands do not, women's intuition. What wives have to say is vitally important, and their husbands need their wise input. Helping them is a very important and necessary role. Wives are to be a sounding board; husbands need their wives' insight and wisdom.

Yet when there is an impasse and a couple cannot reach a decision, then someone needs to make the final call. That is to be the husband, by design—remember that he is accountable to God for those decisions. Wives may not agree with all these decisions, yet they stand behind them. If there are consequences, we must face them together.

I had to get to a place of trusting the Lord in this; it is to Him I do this, even if my husband does not make the best decisions or does not follow the Lord. Husbands *cannot* be in their God-given role of leader if wives are not first willing to follow. And remember, women are submissive in Christ's strength and as unto the Lord, not because they deserve it, necessarily. Women are called to be all that Christ desires of them as women and as wives, in compassion and love, humility, and kindness.

I learned to allow God to work on my husband through my light and witness. See, before that, I wanted to call the shots, which meant we had two dominant personalities head-butting during conflict, both always wanting to be right or have their way. A family cannot successfully grow and develop in love and encouragement with two chiefs vying for control all the time. Over time, I saw huge changes as I got behind my husband and supported him; I became his biggest cheerleader.

Wives, try it and see what this does for your husbands' confidence and well-being. Watch what happens in your husband when you get behind him in this way, from a place of love. Trust me; it changes him from the inside out when you honor and respect him in this way and let him lead. This does not mean, however, following him into something illegal, immoral, or against God's Word. Speak out and up, in love.

> Submit to one another out of reverence for Christ. Wives submit yourselves to your own husbands as you do to the Lord. For the husband is the head of the wife as Christ is the head of the church, His body, of which He is the Savior. Now as the church submits to Christ, so also wives should submit to their husbands in everything. Husbands love your wives, just as Christ loved the church and gave himself up for her to make her holy, cleansing her by the washing with water through the word, and to present her to himself as a radiant church, without stain or wrinkle or any other blemish, but holy and blameless. In this same way, husband's ought to love their wives as their own bodies. He who loves his wife loves himself. After all, no one ever hated their own body, but they feed and care for their body, just as Christ does the church— for we are members of His body. For this reason, a man will leave his father and mother and be united to his wife, and the two will become one flesh. This is a profound mystery—but I am talking about Christ and the church. However, each one of you also must love his wife as he loves himself, and the wife must respect her husband.

> —Ephesians 5:21–33 (NIV)

That the woman was made of a rib of Adam out the side of Adam, not made out of his head to rule over him, nor out of his feet to be trampled upon, but out of his side to be equal to him, under his arm to be protected by him and near to his heart to be beloved. (Henry n.d., 20)

I love this beautiful picture of what God intends for us—not from his head to rule over him, nor from his feet to be trampled on by him, but out of his side—loved and protected by him.

Companionship

Husbands want a companion, someone to have fun with, to share their interests with, even if it is just sitting by his side, watching dirt-bike racing. Richard would prefer me by his side, off-roading or anything else. What does he love to do in which I can get involved with him? We found it helpful to make a list of everything we like to do, see where the overlaps are, and do more of those things together—like his wanting to explore the outdoors quickly and me wanting to explore it slowly. We do some of each and meet in the middle as well.

We love to travel and explore in these ways. Companionship is so important. One day, the kids will be gone. You better have a foundation so you can enjoy spending time together when they leave, or you might be in for real trouble at this stage. On that note, ladies, make sure you have something you are passionate about to get involved in before those kiddos leave home too, especially if you are not working outside the home. This makes the transition into empty-nesting so much smoother. Listen: we dearly love our girls, and we also absolutely love empty-nesting too now.

A man needs to know his wife is content—content with him, with your financial situation, what you have and don't have, and so on. Discontentment breeds trouble. Men are wired to provide and protect. When a wife complains about not having enough and so on, it feels like a direct blow to his pride, which can lead to his feeling like a failure.

References

1. Crabb, Larry. 2013. *The Marriage Builder: Creating True Oneness to Transform Your Marriage*. Grand Rapids, MI: Zondervan Publishing.
2. Graham, Ruth Bell. 1988. *It's My Turn*. New York, NY: Fleming H. Revell.
3. Henry, Matthew. n.d. *An Exposition of the Old and New Testament: with Practical Remarks and Observations*. New York, NY: Fleming H. Revell.

12

LEARNING TO BE CONTENT

> I know what it is to be in need, and I know what it is to have
> plenty. I have learned the secret of being content in any and every
> situation, whether well fed or hungry, whether living in plenty or
> want. I can do all things through Christ who gives me strength.
> —Philippians 4:12–13 (NIV)

I have struggled with comparison and perfectionism extensively over the
years. Both can steal my joy and destroy any chance of contentment. There
will always be someone ahead of me and someone behind me. Comparing
myself to those behind me can lead to pride; comparing myself to those
ahead of me often leads to discontentment, envy, and a lack of gratitude.

> Turns out it doesn't matter a hill of beans how old you
> are, how wise you are, or how you're sitting pretty—the
> more you let yourself compete and compare, the more you
> forget your own calling. (Voskamp 2016)

I am most tempted by comparison in regard to my painting. There are
so many incredible artists. I love to see how they express their own creative
outlets! At the same time, it can be all too easy to covet their skills and
accomplishments, especially when they make it into a prestigious show or
gallery, and I do not—especially when I was certain that I would. There
is a subjective element to a show's or gallery's jury process, and you never
know what they might be specifically looking for. But the sting can be
strong nonetheless. Rejection is just part of the process in the journey of
an artist and in many other areas in life too.

Don't let criticism or rejection stop you from pursuing your passion. Remember, any opinion given by a gallery owner or director is just that, an opinion. (Horejs 2020, 7/2/20)

Maybe it's personal preference; maybe I was not ready. Maybe, as I believe is often the case, the timing was just not right. I pray all the time for God to open the doors and close the doors. Open the doors I am meant to walk through at this time, and close the doors I am not meant to walk through. I seek to pray this way in all life's decisions. I trust in God's timing, plan, and purpose for my life, my relationships, and my work. That's not to say it's easy or that patience isn't difficult at times. Yet I trust in the process that is refining me and my work. And who knows? Maybe my work is meant for somewhere else. The truth is, I have had plenty of success to be thankful for, more and more collectors, awards, and gallery representation. I have been a museum-featured artist, and my work has been juried into prestigious shows. I've had incredible client feedback, press, exposure, and increased activity each year. Everything works out as it should.

I find my way out of comparison by shifting my heart space to one of *gratitude* and *generosity*. I am genuinely happy for the success of others and am thankful for my gifts, talents, and successes with which I've been blessed. I recognize that I am right where I am supposed to be and when I am supposed to be there. Of course, this doesn't mean having goals and working toward them is a bad thing. It means they are fluid and evolving. We work them, grow, evolve, learn, and trust that in the right time and the right way, they will unfold.

I have nothing to prove, so why do I forget sometimes? I am wholly loved for who I am. I am called to be a bringer of light and beauty, bringing hope and encouragement to a hurting world. I am not to strive for approval or be concerned about what people think of my work and words. *Create and release. Let what happens happen*, I hear.

When those pangs of envy flash, this is where I choose to go with them—to wash them out and overcome, to kick them to the curb. They are of no use to me and only cause me more harm than good.

> For I know the plans I have for you, declares the Lord, plans to prosper you and not to harm you, plans to give you a hope and a future.
>
> —Jeremiah 29:11 (NIV)

> No eye has seen, no ear has heard, and no mind has imagined what God has prepared for those who love him.
>
> —1 Corinthians 2:9 (NIV)

I love this. When I read it, I am reminded that what God has for me is so much bigger and better than whatever I can dream up. He has given me my gifts, talents, life experiences, and my marriage for a reason. By drawing close to God, leaning in, and listening, He will open the doors and guide my steps. I need only to trust and step out when and where He leads me.

> For my thoughts are not your thoughts, neither are your ways my ways, declares the Lord. As the heavens are higher than the earth, so are my ways higher than your ways and my thoughts higher than your thoughts.
>
> —Isaiah 55:8–9 NIV)

When God doesn't answer me or direct me in the way I think it should be, Jesus reminds me that He sees so much more than I can ever comprehend. I need to always remember to get my eyes off myself and others and to keep my eyes on Jesus. "Not good enough" is a lie. My gifts and talents now and what they will become are exactly what they are supposed to be.

> When we stop worrying about the end result or final product, we free ourselves to be absorbed in the process and experience the joy of serving the work. (Elsheimer 2012, 101)

I have learned that we will never be truly content until we realize that none of what we have, or strive to be and do, or accomplish will ever fill the void meant to be filled by Christ. He wants all of us—our hearts, our minds, our souls, a personal relationship with Him—by letting Him all the way in. Then we can rest in Him and trust Him to work in and through us in ways we cannot even begin to imagine. This is where true contentment is found, regardless of the situation around us, good or bad. He is with us always. He does not want our striving and our works, our comparisons and perfectionism. He wants us right we're we are, with all our faults and failings. Come as you are.

> You should only compare yourself with your former you. Am I further along than I was last month, last year, five years ago? Contentment is a decision to be content with what God has given me today. (Moore)

What of Perfectionism?

I most want to invoke light and beauty, joy and hope, encouragement and inspiration in my paintings, my stories, and all I do. I want to bring you to another place, capture a memory, cause you to feel and reflect. I pray for this, before and during the painting process. Sometimes, falling into perfectionism can get in the way of this and make me feel stifled.

I read a blog post by Dreama Tolle Perry, "When Is a Painting Finished?":

> If perfection in a painting is not the gold standard for deciding if it is finished, then what is?

> Abandoning the idea of perfection in my work, a relaxing of my "standards." This one single thing was and still is both life changing and life affirming for me. It's me accepting me. With every painting there comes a letting go of my need for perfection. Each letting go brings me a little closer to my one true self. (2017)

I love this! Perry asks the following questions to determine when a painting is complete:

> Does it contain within it that joy I felt while doing it?
> Can I view it and feel a tenderness and kindness towards myself?

Whoa—stop right there. I certainly never thought about it like that. Don't we tend to get critical, looking for what's wrong in a painting or in other areas of our lives? If only I could do better, be better, speak better, write better—the list goes on. None of us is perfect. We were never created to be. Why did I always feel I needed to be perfect? Is it only me? Was it partly the trait of a firstborn or going through pain and struggle as a child and an adult, never feeling worthy? Yes, you need a healthy dose of criticism to grow in your painting and anything else when you strive for excellence. But excellence and perfectionism are two different things.

> "A perfectionist sets unrealistic expectations for themselves and for others ... a perfectionist will let failures get in their head and slow them down."—Monique McLean

> Excellence is obtainable. Excellence will uplift you; perfectionism will make you feel defeated. When you embrace excellence in your life and your business, you are embracing your unique design with the tools and resources you currently have. Grow your strengths, sharpen your gifts and talents. (Perry 2017)

We all have imperfections, haven't we? It's all part of what makes you uniquely you and me uniquely me. Sometimes, we just need to kick perfectionism to the curb and embrace our imperfections. Otherwise, it can steal our joy and contentment. True contentment is trusting and stepping into our plans and purposes and trusting in divine timing.

Dreama Tolle Perry's questions for when a painting is complete continue:

> Does it make me smile? Do I see "me" in it?

It has helped me to realize that my art is not about "wowing" someone else with my skills. It is about bringing some smiles, some truth, some happy to this life while I am here.

If it's not perfect then it is for sure … me. Each time I create I get to choose. A form of contrived perfection OR seeing imperfect me in my work. I choose the imperfections. In exchange, the paintings seem to breathe on their own. They have a sense of liveliness. Paint from your heart, paint with joy, let go of perfection, embrace the beauty of truth in yourself and your art.

When it delivers the emotion you felt. It makes you smile. It feels joy. It is finished. Period.

It's not about perfecting a painting. It's about allowing your heart to maintain the joy from one painting to the next. Not pressing it all out to gain some unrealistic idea of perfect. All of life is abundant with joys, carrying from one moment to the next … let your paintings simply pause and breathe in that joy from one to the next. (2017)

Body Image

Where else have I struggled with perfectionism and comparison? How about body image—I already mentioned this briefly. It's often a difficult thing for most women. There is intense pressure to look a certain way, which can be smothering at times. How easy is it for me to stand in front of the mirror and start tearing down my flaws, looking for everything "wrong" instead of anything right? Do you do this? I see the cellulite, not getting myself into *those* jeans any longer, stretch marks, extra wrinkles, and so much gray, now that I am over fifty. Why do I often feel such a need to look perfect? There it is, isn't it? Signs of those old arrows once again. *I'm not good enough.*

Amanda spoke truth into me when I was doing it again. "Mom, how do you think that makes me feel?" *Oh no! What am I doing? What have I done?* That is the last thing I would want anyone to feel. I don't look at other women's bodies critically, only my own. In fact, I see true beauty inside *and* out in women, regardless of age, size, color, and so on. Amanda helped me to realize that it was not what I was seeing in the mirror; it was the lies I was hearing, that old broken record I've heard over and over again. Well, it was time to break it over my knee and cast it into the fire.

Who cares if I have extra wrinkles, stretch marks, and gray hair? Do these things define me? No! I celebrate me. Thank you, Lord, for the way You have created me, perfect in my imperfections. My heart breaks for the hurt little girl inside of so many women. I want to wrap my arms around her and tell her she is *so* loved, just the way she is, unconditionally. She is beautiful, priceless. You are priceless. There is beauty in aging and in all of the life experiences and wisdom that come along with it.

How Does Jesus See Me?

Jesus showed me my true self, created in His image, wonderfully and fearfully made, completely loved unconditionally, cleansed, forgiven, made whole. He healed my broken heart. I have learned to celebrate my body. There are certainly days when I must remind myself of this, but I do.

I posted the following *NIV Study Bible* footnote to Genesis 1:26 right smack on my dressing mirror:

> Because we bear God's image, we can feel positive about ourselves. Criticizing or downgrading ourselves is criticizing what God has made and the abilities He has given us. Knowing that you are a person of worth helps you love God, know Him personally, and make a valuable contribution to those around you.

And then for Genesis 1:31:

> You are part of God's creation and He is pleased with how He made you.

Mmm, so good. I read this aloud to Richard, and he kissed my forehead gently. "Remember," he said.

Do I still fall into perfectionism for myself and my artwork from time to time? Sure, and it never leads to anything good; it's all a lie. But now, I recognize it. How do I pull myself out? I remember who I am—beloved and cherished in all my beautiful imperfection.

I read a blog post recently about a cancer survivor and people were asking her what she learned through this journey. She shares how self-conscious she always was about her body and her cellulite; never wanted to wear a swimsuit or shorts, especially in public. She wore jeans or dresses for most of the summer. She reflects on how much she missed out on because she wouldn't wear the swimsuit. She stresses that if you want to be in the game, in the action, swimming with the kids before it's too late, then wear it. Who cares if your thighs are your friends or not. She also shares that this is only the beginning. By letting this go you open up more easily to dance like no one is looking, sing loudly, wait on the dishes, skinny dip, let loose, and try new things.

Wow, I *love* this! Lord, help me to live free and playful. Who cares what anyone thinks anyway? Let me see and experience the joy in every single moment, to laugh, and sing, and savor every precious day. And may we all wear that swimsuit.

References

1. Voskamp, Ann. 2016. *The Broken Way: A Daring Path to the Abundant Life*. Grand Rapids, MI: Zondervan.
2. Horejs, Jason. 2020. "How to Overcome Rejection as You Seek Gallery Representation." Red Dot Blog. https://reddotblog.com/how-to-overcome-rejection-as-you-seek-gallery-representation-19-2.
3. Elsheimer, Janice. 2012. *The Creative Call: An Artist's Response to the Way of the Spirit*. Colorado Springs, CO: WaterBrook Press.
4. Moore, Dr Mark. Weekly sermon. Christ Church of the Valley, Peoria, AZ.
5. McLean, Monique. 2016. *"21 Days of Prayer for Your Business."* Safari Technology
6. Perry, Dreama Tolle. 2017. "When Is a Painting Finished?" *Dreama* (blog). https://dreamatolleperry.com/2017/05/when-is-a-painting-finished-part-1.

13

LIVING WITH CHRONIC PAIN AND ILLNESS

Three times I pleaded with the Lord to take it away
from me. But He said to me, "My grace is sufficient for
you, for my power is made perfect in weakness."
—2 Corinthians 12:8–9 (NIV)

At my cabin, I was snuggled up on the couch with my sweet doggies. There was a steady light rain, and with the windows open, the scent of the pines was heavenly.

The rain finally came, after our severe drought. It began the night before and was slow and steady throughout the night; just what we needed. My husband, a friend, and his boys happily worked in the rain, building horseshoe pits. Soon the fun would begin! I fed them well, cleaned up, and started writing again. I loved the beautiful time alone to reflect and write.

Writing about living with chronic pain and illness is no easy topic. Initially, I wasn't sure if I would include this; I didn't want to come across as complaining. Yet this too has been a huge and difficult part of my journey and has taught me much about myself, about the nature of God, and about others who suffer as well. The truth is, it's hard to talk about or explain what living in pain feels like to those who have not walked this road as well. It can be physically and emotionally draining, even debilitating.

Earlier, I mentioned I was diagnosed with IBS in high school and that I've had severe attacks that left me immobilized on a regular basis. These symptoms most often flared under extremely stressful or emotional situations. I have battled this off and on for most of my life, always having to be careful with my gut—my overly sensitive system. Living with chronic illnesses can take a toll on your mind, body, and spirit. It can be extremely exhausting and frustrating, often leaving you in a state of hopelessness. I have lived through a roller coaster of emotions as each of these conditions surfaced and resurfaced again.

Years ago, I had my gallbladder removed and many of my gut symptoms improved. I had unknowingly been battling gallbladder disease for over twenty years. My quality of life became much better—until recently. My gut kicked off again in a horrible way, this time with new and extreme symptoms. I wondered if I, all of a sudden, developed a problem with wine. *Let it not be so!* Was it alcohol, in general? Rich or spicy foods? Gluten? I experimented on my own, trying to figure it out, but came up empty. It didn't seem to matter what I ate or drank. I would bloat immediately and feel cramping and pain, nausea, bowel issues, and a loss of appetite. Once again, I saw specialists and underwent myriad testing, honoring my husband.

The doctor asked why I had waited so long. Thankfully, the scans showed no masses. Next came an endoscopy, with biopsies, colonoscopy, and additional tests. It was best to rule out the most serious conditions. Now that I had, I chose to go with the protocol from my naturopathic MD, and, thankfully, over time, my situation improved.

It is challenging to need to be concerned about everything you eat and drink, where you are going, and how these may impact you. It's hard to be free and spontaneous with these thoughts hovering in your mind.

I also had intense back pain for most of my life. I have been put under for numerous surgeries, seemingly more than I can count. Many of those were due to repeated female issues that have plagued me for years, including various biopsies with these too. Thankfully, they have all been negative for cancer; recently, I had a hysterectomy.

However, my most severe medical issue surfaced several years ago. As we were driving down to Mexico, my left shoulder and neck started hurting badly. In the night, I threw up for no apparent reason, and the next morning, my whole left arm and hand went numb, though not painfully. I thought, *Oh no, could these be the signs of a heart attack?* We researched online for answers and started for the US border. Just after crossing, I called my doctor, who instructed me to take a baby aspirin and get to the hospital.

Upon admission, they ran many tests—my heart and carotid arteries were fine. I was advised to see my primary doctor and to ask for a neurologist referral. The ER doctor said it could be a pinched nerve in my neck, but sometimes, MS presents this way. I thought, *What? Why would you say such a thing?*

While scheduling those appointments and during the long wait, a severe pain, like the jabbing of an ice pick in the base of my skull started. The pain was so intense that I was in tears regularly. My neurologist said he thought it was migraines. I didn't think so, as I had never had them, and this was a constant pain.

Mom has experienced migraines for years, and my daughters have as well. I know they are hereditary, but I had no typical migraine symptoms, like seeing an aura, light sensitivity, or nausea. I only had severe and constant pain and left-side numbness. The neurologist asked me to quit all migraine triggers for six weeks, such as caffeine, alcohol, chocolate, and so on, and he put me on migraine medications. They did nothing for the intense pain, and they also made me a crying, blubbering mess! I *had* to get off them.

This doctor sent me for a brain MRI; when he discussed the results, he said there was an abnormal amount of white matter debris, along with a small *lacunar infarct* (stroke). He felt I could have MS and sent me for a spinal tap (which was horribly painful). It was an extremely scary time for me and my family during the long wait to get results. Time seemed to stand still as we waited. Thankfully, this result was negative as well, and the doctor again made a migraine diagnosis. He said that bad migraines can leave damaged spots on the brain, where the blood supply is cut off and cells die. He said there was no telling how old the infarct was.

I received occipital nerve-block injections and spinal blocks in my neck. These were only briefly helpful. The pain was still intense and would spread down my neck, shoulders, and upper back, making it difficult to turn my head.

A new neurologist said it was not migraines but occipital neuralgia, where the nerve endings are firing off pain signals repeatedly. "But why?" I constantly asked. No one could explain this or the numbness in my left arm and toes. The neurologist started me on a nerve-pain blocker. It was not a narcotic, but it still made me foggy and forgetful. My short-term memory was shot. I kept mentioning this but was not taken seriously.

Finally, I was able to acquire a referral to Barrows Neurological Institute, the world's largest neurological disease treatment and research institution, located in Phoenix. The doctor there sent me for more brain and spine scans. He also was concerned about MS and said my brain scan looked like I had it. After a couple of years with them and many tests, they determined I did not have MS. The diagnosis was occipital neuralgia and some form of complicated migraine syndrome. Apparently, a person can have constant migraines, although I still thought this sounded suspicious. This doctor explained that the brain is complicated, and doctors don't always have the answers.

It was great to have the scary things ruled out, of course, but it was extremely frustrating to receive a lot of I-don't-knows. My doctor said it was just a matter of managing my symptoms for a better quality of life. With higher and higher medication doses, we did finally manage to control my head pain, but this did nothing for my back pain. I had to learn what my triggers were and to avoid them as much as possible. Finally, through my Naturopathic M.D., we were able to wean me off all the drugs and cleanse my system, and eventually, the intense pain subsided, I moved back into my moderate to low levels.

Sleep has often been a struggle as well. My mom has battled sleep issues for over twenty-five years, and I sure didn't want to follow in those footsteps, but it appears that I have. I tried many things, but I didn't want to be on prescription sleep medication. With my doctor, we found something that *usually* works—it affects my serotonin levels—but not always. I often have to add other methods. There are plenty of nights when even these other methods do not work, and I lay awake most of the night. It is so frustrating and exhausting, and it has taken a toll on my body and mind. During sleep is when the body repairs itself, which doesn't happen if you are not sleeping. It's so much harder to deal with the trials of life and relationships when you haven't slept.

How I Have Coped

I have run the gamut of emotions over the years, from frustration, to discouragement, fear, complete exhaustion, sadness, depression, anxiousness, hopelessness, resolve, determination, acceptance, defiance, anger—all of these and back again.

I have yelled at myself, "Quit being such a baby, and just deal with it! Many people have to face much tougher things than you do!" Oh, that's a good one—why do we speak so much harsher to ourselves than anyone else would or than we would consider speaking to another? I realized this was falling into the comparison trap. Was my pain better or worse than someone else? What good was this line of thinking?

It was a battle to live in pain every day. I could not remember what living pain-free felt like. *Have I ever felt it? Do I have terrible genes? Why do I have so many physical problems?* It all seemed so unfair. I prayed, and prayed, and prayed.

Some things were lifted, praise God, and some things were not. It has been a frustrating part of my faith journey at times. Yet it was in these times of severe weakness that I drew *so* close to God, and He taught me and spoke to my heart deeply. Those who suffer chronic pain and illness often end up wrestling with their faith. *I know God heals, so why is He not healing me? Why am I experiencing this?*

Sara Young's blog, "Jesus Calling Devotional," spoke volumes to me, and I have an excerpt posted on my bathroom wall even still:

> Thank Me for the conditions that are requiring you to be still. Do not spoil these quiet hours by wishing them away, waiting impatiently to be active again. Some of the greatest works in My kingdom have been done from sick beds and prison cells. Instead of resenting the limitations of a weakened body, search for My way in the midst of these very circumstances. Limitations can be liberating when your strongest desire is living close to Me.
>
> Quietness and trust enhance your awareness of My Presence with you. Do not despise these simple ways of

serving Me. Although you feel cut off from the activity of the world, your quiet trust makes a powerful statement in spiritual realms. My Strength and Power show themselves most effective in weakness.

How many days has this comforted me? I have read it over and over again, and it brings me a measure of peace. I also think of Paul's teachings and how he learned through all of his trials, persecutions, and joys to be content in all circumstances.

For I have learned to be content whatever the circumstances. I know what it is to be in need, and I know what it is to have plenty. I have learned the secret of being content in any and every situation, whether well fed or hungry, whether living in plenty or in want. I can do all this through Him who gives me strength.

—Philippians 4:11–13 (NIV)

Three times I pleaded with the Lord to take it away from me (the thorn in his side). But He said to me, my grace is sufficient for you, for my power is made perfect in weakness. Therefore, I will boast all the more gladly about my weaknesses, so that Christ's power may rest on me. That is why, for Christ's sake, I delight in weaknesses, in insults, in hardships, in persecutions, in difficulties. For when I am weak, then I am strong.

—2 Corinthians 12:8–10 (NIV)

The part about the "thorn in his side" has been of particular interest to me. Some have speculated it may have been malaria, epilepsy, or something else that was chronic and debilitating. Paul prayed many times for its removal, and so have I. I know God is a healer, and I have witnessed Him heal miraculously many times. But here, I see that He does not always do this. I don't know why. But I know and I trust that He can and will use it for His glory, if I let Him.

A message I recently heard at church comes to mind about Paul's preaching, while he was in chains. Despite them—even because of them—he was possibly more effective. He received greater grace, stronger character, humility, and an ability to empathize with others *instead of physical healing*. The footnote in my *NIV Study Bible* says that it benefited those around him to see God work through him in these situations. Our task is to pray, believe, and trust. When we pray, we must entrust our bodies to God's care. We must recognize that nothing separates us from His love and that our spiritual condition is always more important than our physical condition. Although God does not remove Paul's physical affliction, *he does promise* to demonstrate His power in Paul. The fact that God's power is demonstrated in weakness should give us all courage.

Jesus also cried out:

> Going a little farther, he fell with his face to the ground and prayed, "My Father, if it is possible, may this cup be taken from me. Yet not as I will, but as You will."
>
> —Matthew 26:39 (NIV)

It's more about trust, I think—trusting Jesus in all things, *whether I am healed or not*. Lord, I want to always want the Healer more than the healing. Help me to always remember this. I don't think any of this means giving up or giving in, in a negative sense. I think we need to seek wisdom in knowing our bodies and our limitations, and do whatever we can, whatever it takes, to be as healthy as we can be. We need to know and listen to our bodies and act on these clues accordingly. I also know the body has an amazing ability to heal itself when given what it needs, which includes rest. And we have heard that the state of our health is often tied to the state of our hearts and minds and the way we think as well. How many times do we hear of huge improvements through prayer and meditation, a strong support system, processing and purging emotional hurts, forgiveness, and so on? I believe all these things play a significant role. Our bodies are complicated and are completely tied together with our minds and souls. We cannot separate one from another or only treat one area and expect wholeness.

I try not to talk too much about these struggles. First, people don't want to hear about it all the time; I could come across as a complainer or hypochondriac. I have been there, so has Amanda. Others just don't understand if they have never experienced these kinds of trials. It's important, however, to have a few close people who know what it is like and to talk to them.

I also try not to focus too much on my struggles because when I do, I become overly self-focused on my problems, which makes things worse. I then become even *more* sensitive to and aware of my symptoms. When I get my eyes off myself and onto Jesus and other people—taking a real interest in them, loving them, and serving them—it makes a huge difference in the way I feel. I *can* hurt or feel sick but still be joy-filled and thankful and make a difference in the world and the lives of others, and I can have fun too.

Gratitude and Margin

Shifting to a heart space of gratitude is *huge* as mentioned before. What can I be thankful for, every single day, and count all the little blessings? Where do I see God show up in the little things? I can choose to be thankful for the beautiful sunset or having a good day or a beautiful conversation with someone, and so on.

One thing that helped me immensely was the book I received unexpectedly in the mail. God knew what I needed just then. The friend who sent it, not knowing what I was going through, had followed through on a divine prompting. The book was *One Thousand Gifts* by Ann Voskamp. This was the first and only time I have ever read a book from cover to cover and then immediately started it over again. This started me on my journey of seeking gratitude in all things, even the tough things, as I have learned and grown so much through them.

When I look back on my life, I see that it was through the trials that I learned and grew the most; that I grew closest to the Lord, felt His comfort, and heard His voice. I have also learned to have compassion for those going through physical pain, illness, and suffering in any form—I get it.

I also needed to look at how much my stressful lifestyle—living life with little or no margin in my schedule—had an impact on my overall health. Deep down, I sense, and I know. God never created us to live this way, to run ourselves ragged. Why do my husband and I find it so hard to live with daily and weekly margins? We have recently reclaimed our Sabbath, a day of rest that God knows we desperately need. In fact, I completed a study with the women in the neighborhood church group called *Breathing Room* by Sandra Stanley. She says:

> Our time is limited, so we must limit what we do with our time … When we stop paying attention, we drift … We would be wise to recognize the warning signs that our calendars are drifting towards danger. (2017, 49, 56)

> The prudent see danger and take refuge, but the simple keep going and pay the penalty.

—Proverbs 27:12 NIV

How many times have I been running hard, and my body took me down at a most inopportune time? Clearly, I was not aware of the warning signs. If we won't stop and rest sometimes, we will be made to. While reading *You are Free* by Rebekah Lyons, I journaled, reflecting on this. God wants us resting in Him and abiding in Him, and there, He can nourish and refresh us.

"Is that what being down with all the pain was about, Lord?" I wrote. "But I did not take full advantage of it?"

Take advantage? You are missing the point. Abiding in me is a gift to draw you close to me, I heard.

"Yes, but did I have to be in pain?"

No, but you would have it no other way.

Whoa—what? I suppose it is true that I would not stop and rest at times. Well, it did not feel very "restful," Lord!

It could have been. It still can. Did you grow?

"Yes, Lord."

I did not cause you pain, but I did allow it. All things filter through my hands for your own good and growth and correction.

"I will become fully healed as I abide in You? What if I write *yes*, and it is from me, not You, because that is what I want to hear? What if it is not true and makes others question faith because of it?"

You are not to concern yourself with what others think of when they read your words. Only write, pour it out, and leave the rest to me, I heard strongly.

"Thank you, Lord, this is such a tough thing to do, to turn over that part and leave it with you."

I read from *You Are Free* again by Rebekah Lyons.

> Most of us carry chronic stress for so long we no longer recognize the weight of it. That is why I call it grace when our bodies rebel. It's God's way of saying NO MORE! Eventually we can no longer sustain such a life.

The problem with pain management is that we are managing. What if we are called to acknowledge our pain, to confess our inability to beat it? What if we are called to admit that only God's strength is sufficient. God wants us to reveal our weaknesses, to recognize what traumatizes us and exhausts us, He wants us to confess our wounds and sources of stress and pain, bring them into the light so He can redeem and transform them.

> Mental and emotional healing can take longer than physical healing because emotional pain stays hidden for much longer and has deeper roots. It's hard to deal with what has been hidden and sometimes God has us sit in the emotional pain for weeks, months, or even years before the fullness of healing comes.[1] (2017, 165-166)

I am learning to listen to my body much better now, to know my stressors and triggers and to manage them accordingly. I was reminded of a letter from my sister-in-law, Melinda, a number of years ago, when my pain was very acute. She is such a mighty prayer warrior and is often given a message during those intense prayer sessions. She sent me this letter, sharing what had been laid on her heart while praying for me. This part has stayed with me: *I will heal you little by little, bit by bit. Trust me.* I have

---

[1] Reprinted by permission from Zondervan.

continued to heal little by little, and for this, I am immensely grateful. Whatever may come with my health, I choose to rest in gratitude and hope, keeping my eyes on God, my rock and my redeemer, and to trust that He has got this too. Whether I am fully healed or not, I know that He will use this in my life and the lives of others. All is well with my soul. Amen.

> Joy is not the absence of darkness; it is the confidence that it will lift.[2] (Lyons 2017, 188)

The verses of a song by Elevation Worship, "Do it Again," drift through my mind.

> Walking around these walls
> I thought by now they'd fall
> But You have never failed me yet
> Waiting for change to come
> Knowing the battle's won
> For You have never failed me yet
> Your promise still stands
> Great is Your faithfulness, faithfulness.

References

1. Lyons, Rebekah. 2017. *You Are Free*. Grand Rapids, MI: Zondervan.
2. Stanley, Sandra. 2017. *Breathing Room: A 28-Day Devotional for Women*. Georgia, USA: North Point Ministries.
3. Young, Sarah. 2012. "Jesus Calling Devotional." Jesus Calling (blog). https://jesuscalling-today.blogspot.com/2012/02/jesus-calling-by-sarah-young-21612.html.

---

[2] Reprinted by permission from Zondervan.

14

WHAT ABOUT MY HUSBAND?

It's never too late to be who you were meant to be.
—George Elliot

Are you wondering what was going on in Richard all this time? I intentionally delayed this part of the story because it was important to focus on myself and what *I* needed to look at, work on, and change first. What does God want to reveal in my own heart? And at the same time, I needed to lay my husband at the feet of Jesus and trust God to work on his heart as well.

Richard was under his own transformational process. It was a long, raw, and painful process—a lot of three steps forward, two steps back. But he never gave up; he fought through—fought for a relationship with Christ and for our marriage restoration, and our family. He continued seeking counseling and mentoring. We made church and our neighborhood group Bible study a priority. We continued reading together, discussing, and growing in our faith.

He grew stronger day by day. A softness entered his heart, one filled with compassion as he learned to see people through Christ's eyes. There was a humbling in spirit and a tenderness growing within him. He also recognized the need to get his eyes off me and what I was doing or not doing and to work on *his* relationship with Christ.

Men Really Do Have Fragile Hearts

Underneath all the tough and burly exteriors, men really do have fragile hearts. Theirs are pierced just as easily as women's; they are just taught to stuff it and not show the emotion, regardless of how it hurt or damaged them. Deep down in a man's soul, he wants to know if he has what it takes—*Am I good enough?* Men often look for these answers and affirmation or approval, whether they are conscious of this or not. I learned Richard had a similar issue as I had—a deep-rooted need to be accepted by others and to receive their approval, especially from the opposite sex. Boy, both of us with this same issue sure put us in a bad spot. He also had to learn it is only the Lord who meets and fulfils those deepest needs; fills that God-shaped hole in his heart.

Husbands need to feel respected and needed by their wives in all ways, including intimately. These are the ways they feel truly loved. Most men want to be good husbands and want to please their wives; they just aren't always sure how to do this. Men feel they can take on the world when their wives love them by honoring and respecting them, helping them, having fun playing together, and meeting their intimate needs. They need to be truly desired by their wives. Their wives can build them up and send them out into the world, protected in this way, or tear them down, weakening them. Women have a choice.

Dr. Kevin Leman, an internationally known psychologist and award-winning author, has said, "A man needs to feel your respect in order to love you the way you want to be loved. If he does not feel your respect, he won't climb out of his turtle shell to risk loving you because he might get hurt." (Leman 2009, 39)

Communication

My husband learned to communicate on deeper levels. I learned about his own brokenness, his own insecurities and wounds like never before, as well as his wants, goals, and dreams. He took baby steps at first to talk this deeply. As he saw that he could trust me with these thoughts and feelings, our communication grew even deeper. As a wife, you cannot judge or criticize what he shares or its validity if you want him to feel comfortable with you and to share regularly. Are you a safe place for him to come and share his heart? Do you keep what he shares confidential? Can he trust you with whatever he tells you? Just as much as wives need their hearts protected, husbands need their hearts protected too.

Richard and I both learned to honor each other in the way we speak about each other, whether the other person is present or not. He or I might not be listening, but Jesus is.

Don't say anything about your spouse—or anyone else, for that matter—if you would not say it with the person sitting right next to you. Never bad-mouth your spouse to coworkers, family, or friends, and especially not to your children.

My husband had to learn more about me, to study me and what makes me tick. How could he show me the love I need; how could he help me, serve me, and put my needs first, as I did the same for him? We are not perfect; we make plenty of mistakes, but watch what happens in your marriage when you both do these things. Listen, there is no such thing as giving fifty/fifty in a marriage; this simply does not work. One will always measure the other and we are a poor judge of distance. Marriage is about giving all of you, to love and serve your spouse, putting his or her needs before your own. This is what unconditional Christlike love is all about.

I have moved closer to center, and so has he. I have learned not to be so serious and structured and not to have every little thing planned out; to be freer and more spontaneous; to laugh and play. My husband has learned to value the planning when it is called for, to value and seek my wisdom and insight; he puts much weight on what I have to say and seeks it out. He has also learned to see the beauty all around him; to stop and take notice of it and even point it out to me. I love this in him. We work together as a team, hand in hand, step by step, side by side.

But wait—I jumped to the present again.

I also learned men definitely don't like to be told what to do or how to feel, like they are being talked down to or corrected. They sure don't like "you should"—you should do this, and you should do that. Even if I meant nothing confrontational about it, he would perceive it as being told what to do—even when I thought I was helping as well. Boy, I have tried to strike "you should" from my vocabulary completely. My grown daughters don't like it either. Do I? No, I don't.

Spiritual Leader

Little by little, my husband finally started shifting into the role of spiritual leader of our home, as he was designed to be. I had prayed for this, year after year, sometimes questioning if it would ever happen. When this starts to happen, ladies, rejoice. But I had to let go of those reins too. How could he step into that role if I still called all those shots? It's a tough habit to break when you have been there as long as I was. But he cannot lead if you are not willing to follow and have his back.

Richard has always been generous. As his faith grew, God strongly laid on his heart for us to actually tithe, to trust God with our money, not just our made-up definition of what we wanted the tithe to be. Our tithing and giving has been a journey that has evolved along with our faith journey. We had been giving away 10 percent of our income, and the tithe was *inclusive* of all giving. Funny how when your income gets larger and larger, sometimes it can be tougher to give that percentage when looking at the total dollar amount. We shifted to bringing the whole tithe first into the storehouse—our local church. Yes, we completely and totally trust their open-book stewardship. All other giving was above and beyond, and this increased substantially as well.

We had the enormous honor to partner with God and bless some special friends, who had been trying to get pregnant, with the financial means to do in vitro fertilization treatments. Then, we were able to walk beside this couple and welcome a miracle—a beautiful baby boy—into their lives. Thank you, Jesus, for allowing us to be a part of this.

The more we sought to give when it was laid on our hearts, the more seemed to return to us. This is in no way a prosperity teaching; you should never give, *expecting* to receive financially. Sometimes, the blessings received are financial, and sometimes, they are in other areas, like relationships, opportunities, and so on. There is no limit. You give from the heart because you are led and prompted to do so, not because you expect anything in return.

Give, and it will be given to you. A good measure, pressed down, shaken together and running over, will be poured into your lap. For with the measure you use, it will be measured to you.

—Luke 6:38 (NIV)

One thing we have learned is that you *cannot* outgive God. He has proven this time and time again. Another evolution for us was that Richard felt strongly that anything that touched our hands, we tithed on, regardless of the circumstances. It has always been easier for him than me to move to the next level of generosity. Here is a big example: our contracting business is an LLC—all the tax liability funnels through to our personal returns, yet most of the money is left in the company for operating costs. Well, the company does a distribution to us to pay the quarterly taxes for the portion that the company generates. We are, in essence, a funnel; this money then goes straight to the IRS. Richard wanted to tithe on this. *What?* This made no sense to me. Why would we do this?

"I feel led to do this, and we are to trust God in this," he said.

And so we did.

That first year, as our tax returns were completed, we ended up owing only 90 percent of what was distributed. Only God. We have faithfully continued this every year, and one way or another, it has always worked out. Always. I am not saying this is some kind of tithing rule for anyone else to follow. This is just what we have been led to do for us personally. We even tithed on the sale of our house and the old cabin, which were paid off, but we sold at a big loss from when we bought them. We stepped out in faith and did it anyway. You *cannot* outgive God, and He uses this to impact the lives of so many others. I can't begin to tell you all the amazing things that continue to happen for us, both financially and otherwise. Jesus says:

Whoever can be trusted with very little can also be trusted with much, and whoever is dishonest with very little will also be dishonest with much.

—Luke 16:10 (NIV)

We even tithe on little things, like when Richard sells some of his "toys", and over time, we have increased our tithe and additional giving percentage each year, giving progressively. We were not blessed to this degree merely for our own consumption. If we don't make a difference in the world around us, in our community, and in those placed on our hearts, then why do we have all this anyway? God is so faithful. He *always* stretches what is leftover.

As spiritual leader, Richard also initiates prayer with me each morning. Occasionally, we forget, but can I tell you how impactful this is in a marriage? It is so incredibly powerful to pray together.

> For where two or three gather in my name, there am I with them.
>
> —Matthew 18:20 (NIV)

I get to hear his heart, and he gets to hear my heart. Men, do you have any idea what praying together would mean to your wife? Everything. I challenge you to pray sincerely together each day, for thirty days, and see what a difference it makes in your marriage.

> The truth is, when you actively listen to each other in prayer, you are able to empathize at the deepest, most honest level. You are putting yourself in your spouse's shoes. Prayer becomes a much more significant experience when you are listening carefully to the burdens your spouse is repeatedly bringing to the Lord so that you can join him or her in praying for those same things, as well. This can only happen, of course, when each of you is willing to honestly verbalize what's on your heart, when prayer is not a routine exercise devoid of real-life substance and content, when prayer becomes your heart's genuine cry before the Father. Only then can you go to the Lord God almighty together—with both humility and confidence—asking the Lord to encourage your wife when she feels like a failure as a mom or asking God to grant your husband

increased wisdom when he struggles to be the leader of your family. (Rainey 2007, devotion for 6/29)

My husband has continued to lead our neighborhood group Bible study for many years, with me assisting. I love to listen to him teach, share, and challenge through the messages we study. He has led a small Bible study for his guys at work also. What a huge opportunity to reach and challenge these men to be the men they are called to be—the husbands, the fathers, the leaders.

Richard has such a passion for men—helping them to not make the mistakes he has, to lead and teach them, and to come alongside them. He also is drawn to men who are like he was—maybe business owners or at a high level in another capacity, who feel alone, with no one to talk to or ask questions of. We both have a passion for marriages, including leading and hosting marriage retreat weekends. In fact, after returning from his Israel trip, he had even more clarity on what God would have him do in mentoring men. I was thrilled to see what God had in store for Richard. I always knew he had big plans for my husband—always. I look forward to seeing this continue to unfold for him and for both of us together.

References

1. George Eliot. AZQuotes.com, Wind and Fly LTD, 2021. https://www.azquotes.com/quote/844648, accessed August 31, 2021.
2. Rainey, Dennis, and Barbara Rainey. 2007. *Moments with You: Daily Connections for Couples*. Ventura, CA: Bethany House.

15

Life Is but a Journey (In My Husband's Words)

I asked Richard if he would like to share anything. I am eternally grateful to share his words:

When Lucy started talking about writing a book about her life's experiences, I thought, *This will be good for her.* To be honest, I had some fears of dredging up past hurts and the poor decisions I have made. I have lived a life that has been full of twists and turns. I look back on some of these decisions and think, *Why would anyone do that?* The truth is, I wanted to be liked. I wanted to be picked. I wanted those around me to look up to me. For the longest time, I made decisions based on what I selfishly wanted at the time or what I thought it would take to be the cool guy, the guy others would look up to, the one who others would want to be like. The decisions I made were not all bad; some were good, and some helped others, but most came from a place of selfishness; I cared very little for how they affected others.

When I was young child, I was in my dad's old truck, and as I looked around, I thought, *There is too much in this world for it not to have been created by God.* Although I did not have a complete understanding of Christ, I didn't have a hard time believing that He existed. That was about the extent of my belief. God is real, Christ is real, now on to me. How do I get whatever I want at this moment in time? What makes me happy, regardless of how it makes anyone else feel or affects them?

My life has had several crossroads, plenty of wake-up calls, plenty of chances to make the right decisions and turn things around. But for the first forty years of my life, I tended to straighten up just long enough to get things going in the right direction, only to slowly drift back to where I had previously been. I was making decisions that mainly revolved around me or what I thought would make me the life of the party.

It was after our marriage was on the brink of failure that I thought, *I am tired of living my life as a lie.* I was tired of pretending or hiding who I truly was. Most people saw me as a successful, happy guy. The truth was that I was a depressed, scared, lonely man who was looking for acceptance. I wanted to escape. I was tired of living this way.

Lucy *refused* to allow me to just check out. She challenged me, stressing that if I really wanted my life to be different, I needed to find men with whom I could be honest and who I could trust. Three men came to mind. My neighborhood group leader Mike, my dad, and my older brother. I contacted all three and completely opened up. It was the first time that I had been 100 percent honest with anyone. It was freeing, like a huge boulder had been lifted off my shoulders. I began meeting with my brother, Ron, weekly and started to read my Bible daily. Slowly, I understood that asking for forgiveness is only part of the solution. I must also repent, turn and go the other way, and let Christ all the way in. Only through repenting can true forgiveness be achieved.

You have to definitively make a choice to fight for what is yours. We end up in places like this because of hiding the truth from those God has intentionally placed in our lives to help carry burdens too heavy for us to carry on our own. When we live our lives by deceiving those we love, it is only a matter of time before it all comes crashing down—and it did for me.

You need to decide who you are going to serve. For me, it was finally an easy decision. I chose to set aside the lies I had carried my entire life and to start down the path of seeking an honest relationship with Christ and my wife. Although the decision was easy, the journey has not been. At no time in the Bible does Christ say that following Him will be easy, but the rewards we receive while here on this planet are beyond measure.

Here are the steps I took:

1. Met in person with three men whom I knew to be strong in their faith. I was 100 percent honest and transparent with them and confessed my sin. Through that, I selected one to mentor me and hold me accountable.

2. Started counseling. I selected a strong Christian counselor who was qualified to guide me through what I was dealing with. I chose to be transparent with him and not hide anything. Only then could he actually help me.
3. Started studying scripture daily to learn who Christ was and is with a purpose. I tried to gain an understanding of what being a Christian actually meant and to understand why I believed what I said I believed. Just because I went to church and was baptized did not necessarily make me a Christian. Was that all part of my cover story to hide who I was?
4. Repented. I took a look at the path that I was on and chose to turn and go in the opposite direction. I sought to reconcile with my wife and to be the husband she deserved and the father my daughters deserved.

God has revealed much to me through His Word. I have learned that the hole I had in my heart could be filled only with one thing—the love of Christ. *He* picked me. He picked me to be on His team. I look back and wish I would have made different decisions in my life, that I would have woken up earlier, that I wouldn't have hurt all those I have. But I also understand that God gave me free will, and along with free will comes consequences. I trust that even my poor choices can be used to help me to come alongside the other men God has placed around me, to be relatable. I have been exposed to much. God has placed me in numerous painful and beautiful situations and has given me a foundation to help others.

Don't get me wrong—I have not yet arrived, and I am still on this journey. I still make mistakes and deal with my own selfish desires, but I recognize that Christ has chosen me to come alongside my wife, my daughters, and men from all different walks of life. He has chosen me to point others to Him. I strive to do this in the decisions I make and the actions I take. I know that by honoring Him, I am on the path for which I was created.

When Ron began mentoring me, he pointed out that I have always been a leader. People follow me, whether it is in business or friendships. The question is, "Where are you going to lead them?" This has stuck with me ever since.

Two mottos that speak truth to me come to mind: "Every saint has a past, and every sinner has a future," and "Thank God I am not the man I used to be." I hold on to each of them.

My life verse is Psalm 32:1–5 for the way it changed my life.

> Blessed is the one whose transgressions are forgiven, whose sins are covered.
> Blessed is the one whose sin the LORD does not count against them and in whose spirit is no deceit.
> When I kept silent, my bones wasted away through my groaning all day long.
> For day and night your hand was heavy on me; my strength was sapped as in the heat of summer.
> Then I acknowledged my sin to you and did not cover up my iniquity.
> I said, "I will confess my transgressions to the LORD."
> And You forgave the guilt of my sin. (NIV)

When I look at the last fourteen years of my life and the place my marriage is now, it is a true testimony to "life is better with Christ." Lucy and I have a lasting friendship that has been built on a firm foundation. We love spending time together. We laugh together, cry together, pray together, read together, worship together, and serve together. God has absolutely blessed me with an amazing woman. Christ has entrusted me with a huge responsibility to lead my wife, our daughters, and those He has placed around me. I understand this now. As I said, I am still on this journey. I still make mistakes, but Christ not only filled the hole I had in my heart, but He also gave me His heart when I surrendered mine.

16

STAY THE COURSE

I have fought the good fight, I have finished
the race, I have kept the faith.
—2 Timothy 4:7 (NIV)

My children will not remember the words of wisdom I've passed
along over the years, nor will yours remember the good advice you've
given. However, etched in their minds and planted in their hearts is a
permanent picture of who you are and how you lived before them.
—Dorothy Kelly Patterson

I have found it is in Christ and the work of the Holy Spirit within me that
I find my strength and worth. He shows me what lies I have believed and
held onto, and He teaches me how to lay them down. Jesus shows me how
to combat those lies through His Word, prayer, and putting on my armor
and by showing me I am beloved, cherished, whole, and not lacking. I was
created for a purpose, special and unique. He shows me truth. He knew
me before I was born and knitted me together in my mother's womb. Jesus
shows me that He has a plan and a purpose for my life and my gifts and
talents. As I trust in Him and seek Him in all things, these plans unfold,
and the right doors open for me. I have learned to trust in His timing and
not my own. It is laying my worries and dreams down and knowing that
when I am weak, He is strong, and He goes before me. He is working in
ways I can hardly imagine. It is about servant leadership and a humble
heart. This does not mean I don't work hard and grow my talents and
skills, but that I seek Him in all things, and He will make my path straight.

Rest in Him. Listen. My confidence is in Jesus. We need to learn to
stop striving to earn approval from Him and others. We are worthy, loved,

cherished, and important. We are God's children, and we are saved by grace and not by works.

In studying 1 Corinthians 13, the love chapter, the following thoughts came to me: God's love is larger than we can comprehend. It bears all things, loves all things, covers all things, hopes all things, and never fails. God is not an angry dictator, punishing us for all of our mistakes, as many view him. He is not a distant God. He is a loving Father who wants to live in you as you live in Him, a holy communion. This is not to say He doesn't discipline us at times—and sometimes harshly. Why do you correct your own children? It is because you love them so much and want to train and teach them; you only want what is best for them. How much greater is the Lord's love for us? Often, He tries to get our attention, over and over again, as we see in the Old Testament. Repeatedly, God spoke clearly on how He would have the Israelites live, knowing what was best and healthiest. He longed for an intimate relationship with them (and with us). Time and time again, the Israelites turned their backs on Him and disobeyed.

God was so patient; He warned many times of consequences, which were ignored. The Israelites were given every opportunity to turn from their ways. He encouraged them to repent and return; they would not, and He disciplined them or allowed the consequences of their own actions to occur. Why? To remind them that He is Lord of all and wanted to live in relationship with them because of His great love. In him, we are to put our trust, our hope, our faith, and obedience, out of our own love and reverence for our Lord and gratitude for His mercy and grace.

God repeatedly tried to get *our* attention, trying to show Richard and me the danger signs and red flags. We were faced with one wake-up call after another, from liver cancer and illness, to a motorcycle accident, marital issues, trauma, and natural disasters. He kept trying to draw us close to him and, at times, warn us where our behavior, lifestyle, and the state of our hearts was heading. Like the Israelites, we were blind to it all; we were caught up in our own selfish pursuits. But God knew what it would take to bring us in; what it would take for us to finally see the light, to bring us to our knees and back to Him. Thank you, Jesus!

Often we ask if every bad thing that happens is us being disciplined, God causing something to happen because we did something wrong? Absolutely not! Sometimes, it is simply consequences of our own poor choices or the poor choices of others—free will. Sometimes, it is spiritual warfare. And sometimes, it is so God can demonstrate His power in our lives.

In John 9:1-3, Jesus's disciples asked him,

> "Rabbi, who sinned, this man or his parents that he was born blind?" "Neither this man nor his parents sinned," Jesus said, "but this happened so that the work of God might be displayed in his life."

Jesus then went on to heal the blind man. I have learned that He does not make all these bad things happen to us, but they do all filter through His hands. Can He stop it from happening? Yes, and sometimes He does, through our prayers and the prayers of others. Other times, He does not, for some greater purpose. As I said, He knew exactly what it would take to bring us in. He brought us to a place where we could do nothing in our own strength. Finally, we laid it at His feet in surrender and trust, knowing His great love for us. We asked Him to come into our hearts and move in our lives; we gave up control. Was this failure? No, I think this is why we fought it for so long. From a worldly perspective, it can sometimes feel like failure, but it is not. It is allowing God to fill us with His strength, love, peace, wisdom, and guidance and to bring us through to the other side. It is when we give it all up to Jesus and don't take it back that we free His hands to work in our situations, our lives, and our marriages.

Regardless of why bad things happen to us, God can redeem and work in and through all of our circumstances to build our faith and our character. When have you grown the most? Was it in times when things were smooth sailing or walking through the valley, finally emerging on the other side?

I know my answer. For me, there is no question. Through all the trials in my life, I have learned to lean on God. It was in those times that I grew closer to Him and learned the most. I have found that He often does His greatest work in my life in the midst of trial and adversity. It's very powerful to ask the question, "God, what are You trying to teach me through this situation?" If you seek the answer earnestly, He will answer you and stretch you, lead you and guide you.

It's difficult, however, to give thanks and praise to God for the storm, and when you're in the storm, to know that He has a plan and a purpose and that He will bring you through. Often, we need to look back and see what He has already brought us through to give us the courage to thank Him in the midst of the storm, trusting there is purpose in it and He will see us through to the other side.

God uses our trials in powerful ways to transform our lives and, through us, the lives of those around us. I think that is why Paul says to be thankful in times of trial; we know that God is working for our greater good and will carry us through, even if we don't understand how or why. He loves us so much. He loves *you* so much. He chose you and me. I pray you receive this deeply into your heart. Take a chance; it will prove fruitful.

You see, no matter what you are going through or have gone through, no matter what you have done or has been done to you, you can be redeemed. You can be made whole, washed clean, and begin again anew. You can choose to put a stake in the ground and do things differently. Every day is a new day. What will you choose today?

> Our Savior kneels down and gazed upon the darkest acts of your lives. But rather than recoil in horror He reaches out in kindness and says, 'I can clean that, and from the basin of His grace scoops a palm full of mercy and washes our sin. (Lucado 2012, 36)

You are not your past, your regrets, or your pain. All that was intended to harm, God intended for good. His arms have you.

> Jesus is drawn to the broken parts of us we would never want to draw attention to. Jesus is the most attracted to the busted and sees the broken as the most beautiful. And our God wants the most unwanted parts of us. Nothing pleases God more than letting Him touch the places you think don't please him. God is drawn to broken things, so He can draw the most beautiful things. (Voskamp 2016, 150)

Many of us believe the lie that we are too damaged to be completely healed, but nothing is impossible with Christ. No one is too far gone.

> Therefore, if anyone is in Christ, he is a new creation the old has passed away; behold, the new has come.
>
> —2 Corinthians 5:17 (ESV)

> And I am sure of this, that he who began a good work in you will bring it to completion at the day of Jesus Christ.
>
> —Philippians 1:6 (NIV)

Amen to that! Praise God, You will finish what You started in me.

Remember that we are not meant to do life alone but in community with others—leading, guiding, loving, helping, serving, and supporting each other. Our tendency is to withdraw in times of trouble, to hide out and isolate. I had to fight this temptation and find the courage to step out and seek help, to let someone come alongside me. Find a godly mentor or one who will speak truth to you. God loves to use other people to work in your life, and He wants to use you to impact another. Will you let Him use you? Will you be is hands and feet?

I think again of the message my mom sent to me as I started this book:

> Your story could be the key that unlocks someone else's prison. Don't be afraid to share it. —unknown

Lord, let it be true for me; may my story be a key.

What about you? Are you willing to share your story? We all have one; each of us can impact the life of another in a powerful way if we just step out in courage and faith and share it when we are prompted.

What If

What if the trials you have walked through had purpose? What if all the pain of what you have done or what has been done to you happened to draw you close to God, to show you your great need for Him? What if it was to teach and train, to strengthen you, to build your character and your resolve? What if it was to give you a story, a powerful story, a testimony? What if God wanted to use you and your story in a mighty way to help others? What if you chose to truly surrender, letting God all the way in, dropping the walls, choosing to trust, and walking with Him in all ways? What great power might be released in and through you when you do?

I am so thankful for my broken story, for our story, and the ministry God has given us. Amen.

My Marriage and Family Today

Today, Richard and I are each other's closest confidant and best friend. What a beautiful thing it is to be this intimately connected in this way. It's hard to believe it took almost twenty years of marriage to get here. Now, after celebrating our sweet thirty-third anniversary, he continues to be my best friend and lover. What if I had thrown in the towel, given in, and given up? Where would we be now? Where would our daughters be? Look at all of the incredible blessings and memories we would have missed. To get here it took us both, each choosing to put a stake in the ground and choose to live life differently, to fight for our marriage.

Richard and Lucy's twenty-fifth anniversary vow renewal

Dr. Don Wilson has said, "When your spouse knows you will always be there, no matter what, this is the biggest indicator of a successful marriage."

Each of us brings our own set of flaws with us when we marry and unfortunately, we add new ones as time goes along. But marriage should be the best place for two imperfect people to find acceptance and ongoing forgiveness ... as well as the courage to change and grow. (Rainey 2007, devotion for 6/9)

It's like the Jason Gray song, "If You Want to Love Someone":

If you want to love someone
Search their soul for where it's broken
Find the cracks and pour your heart in ...

The heart will hide where it's been broken
But the fault lines still remain
Like a map to lead you home when
You can enter through their pain

Father, let us always be a light and a witness in marriage and in all we do, even when we have no idea who is watching. May we always keep each other the highest priority, behind only you, safeguarding our relationship.

My daughters have such a deep, beautiful, loving relationship with their dad now, and with me as well. This took a whole lot of time and intentionality on Richard's part, as he proved who he is now and his trustworthiness, and he demonstrated how much he loved them. They talk often and seek him out for wise counsel for many of life's situations. And they are all still silly and playful together; this brings my heart much joy. We laugh together often at all the silly comments and expressions, and especially when Richard breaks out with the River Dance reserved for only us. We laugh until our sides burst! I am deeply thankful for these moments and for the beautiful relationship we all have today.

Dickens family, 2019

My Father, I cannot begin to thank You enough for what You have done in my life and my husband's life and for where You have brought us in you. Thank You for redeeming and restoring my marriage; it is truly a miracle. Thank You for my beautiful, talented, hardworking, fun-loving girls. Thank You deeply, Lord, that I get to be their mom. Thank You for calling me to create and for inspiring others through my paintings and writing. May I recede and You go forth through them. Thank You for blessing our finances that we may be a blessing to so many others and for teaching us how to responsibly use our money.

Thank You for our health, Lord, and for patience and contentment as I wait upon you. Thank You for the ability to explore your creation. Thank You for giving me strength when I am weary and for giving me a joyful and appreciative heart. Thank You for giving me the courage to share my journey. I am sorry it has taken so long. Yet your timing is always perfect, isn't it? This is what You have been preparing me to do; I see this clearly now. Last, Lord, I thank You for every person reading these pages. May they know it is *not* by mistake, or by chance. May their hearts be encouraged. May you meet them here, right where they are. Amen.

My great hope and prayer in sharing my journey with you is that you will find and experience hope. We are nothing without hope. I pray that you will see others through the eyes of grace and that you can see those in your life through the eyes of grace as well, including yourself. I pray you will meet Jesus in my story and my husband's because His story is woven through ours. It was in putting Him first in our hearts and lives and in the center of our marriage that truly changed *everything*. God bless!

> Those who hope in the Lord will renew their strength. They will soar on wings like eagles; they will run and not grow weary; they will walk and not be faint.

—Isaiah 40:31 (NIV)

References

1. Dorothy Kelley Patterson. AZQuotes.com, Wind and Fly LTD, 2021. https://www.azquotes.com/author/52179-Dorothy_Kelley_Patterson, accessed August 31, 2021.
2. Lucado, Max. 2012. *Just like Jesus: A Heart like His.* Nashville, TN: Thomas Nelson.
3. Voskamp, Ann. 2016. *The Broken Way: A Daring Path to the Abundant Life.* Grand Rapids, MI: Zondervan.
4. Rainey, Dennis, and Barbara Rainey. 2007. *Moments with You: Daily Connections for Couples.* Ventura, CA: Bethany House.
5. Wilson, Don. Weekly sermon. Christ Church of the Valley, Peoria, AZ.

Afterword

Refined by Fire

We can be delivered from the fire, and our faith is built. We can be delivered through the fire, and our faith is refined. We can be delivered by the fire into His arms, and our faith is perfected.

—Mark Moore

I have experienced great growth in coming through the other side of my own fiery trials. In these times, I have purged the old, learned much, and grown the closest to God. Through these trials, I have learned to trust God completely, regardless of my circumstances and regardless of His answering my prayers in the way I want them answered. There is mighty power in prayer; prayer moves mountains. I have experienced this over and over again. These witnessed miracles are embedded deeply in my heart.

Pray without ceasing; pray fervently. Sometimes, we need to look back to recognize what God has brought us through, as this encourages us for a current trial.

There are times when a prayer is not answered in the way we hoped. It boils down to a matter of trust. Will I trust God completely, regardless of the outcome—even if I am not healed, even if I am not rescued from a particular situation, even if my marriage is not restored? Will I trust that God knows what He is doing, more so than I do; that He sees all, knows all, and has my best interest at heart?

Yes, Lord, I do. Even though I don't know how my situations will work out, I know You *always* bring me through to the other side, and there is blessing when I reach it.

I am reminded of the story in Daniel of Shadrach, Meshach, and

Abednego, which was shared by our teaching pastor Mark Moore. These young Jews were taken into exile by King Nebuchadnezzar. The king's strategy was to completely strip away their identities, including their faith and trust in God, and to cause them to lose hope. He was trying to persuade them to follow foreign gods. Yet of all the Jews, it was these men who stood strong in their faith and trust in God; they would not falter. The king had a large gold statue erected and commanded all to bow before it and worship him. These men refused to bow. The king was angered greatly and threatened to throw them into the burning furnace. Still, they stood their ground.

> King Nebuchadnezzar, we do not need to defend ourselves before you in this matter. If we are thrown into the blazing furnace, the God we serve is able to deliver us from it, and He will deliver us from your Majesty's hand. *But even if He does not*, we want you to know, Your Majesty, that we will not serve your gods or worship the image of gold you have set up.
>
> —Daniel 3:16–18 (NIV, italics added)

God rescued these men from the fiery furnace, and the course of history was changed. The key here is their words before—*even if He chooses not to*, we will not bow down. We will trust our God. We will stand strong. Even if Shadrach, Meshach, and Abednego had burned to ashes, they would have immediately entered heaven and Christ's loving arms.

> I know You're able and I know You can
> Save through the fire with Your mighty hand
> But even if You don't
> My hope is You alone
>
> —"Even If" by Mercy Me

When traveling through the fire, healing takes time. Hang in there; it will come. After a forest fire, the seedlings punch through the charred forest floor and emerge as the most beautiful wildflowers, vibrant and free. They sway in the breeze, reaching up toward the sun. Everything is new once again. Seasons come and seasons go, yet light always follows the darkness. The promise of spring comes once again.

References

1. Moore, Dr. Mark. Weekly sermon. Christ Church of the Valley, Peoria, AZ.

SUGGESTED READING LIST

1. *The Circle Maker*, Mark Batterson
2. *I Thought I'd Be Done by Now: Hope and Help for Mothers of Adult Children Searching for Peace*, Wendy Boorn, MC, LPC
3. *Streams in the Desert*, Mrs. Charles E. Cowman (L. B. Cowman)
4. *Different by Design*, Rodney Cox
5. *Love and Money*, Rodney Cox
6. *The Creative Call*, Janice Elsheimer
7. *Just Like Jesus: Learning to Have a Heart Like His*, Max Lucado
8. *You Are Free*, Rebekah Lyons
9. *Core 52*, Mark E. Moore
10. *Moments with You*, Dennis and Barbara Rainey
11. *Fervent*, Priscilla Shirer
12. *Breathing Room Devotional*, Sandra Stanley
13. *The Broken Way*, Ann Voskamp
14. *One Thousand Gifts*, Ann Voskamp

Check out Lucy's author website at www.LucyDickensAuthor.com and her artist website: www.LucyDickensFineart.com. Follow her on Facebook and Instagram.

Photo Credits

Chapter 1

Photo 1, Lucy age 5: by Butch Brown

Photo 3, Santa: by Mary Schulte

Photo 4, Lucy and Jason: by Butch Brown

Photo 5, modeling: by Johnnie Welborn

Chapter 2

Photo 7 wedding photo: by Butch Brown

Chapter 16

Photo vow renewal: by Drew Brashler

CPSIA information can be obtained
at www.ICGtesting.com
Printed in the USA
LVHW112315090422
715422LV00004B/9